Simply Incredible Bulletin Boa

Amy Vangsgard

Alleyside Press®

Fort Atkinson, Wisconsin

Published by Alleyside Press, an imprint of Highsmith Press LLC
Highsmith Press
W5527 Highway 106
P.O. Box 800
Fort Atkinson, Wisconsin 53538-0800
1-800-558-2110

© Amy Vangsgard, 1998

The paper used in this publication meets the minimum requirements of
American National Standard for Information Science — Permanence of
Paper for Printed Library Material. ANSI/NISO Z39.48-1992.

Library of Congress Cataloging-in-Publication Data

   Vangsgard, Amy.
     Simply incredible bulletin boards / Amy Vangsgard.
       p. cm.
     Includes bibliographical references.
     ISBN 0-917846-98-2 (alk. paper)
     1. Bulletin boards. 2. Authors--Study and teaching.
   3. History--Study and teaching. I. Title.
     LC1043.58.V33 1998
371.33 ' 56--dc21   97-49417
                                     CIP

Contents

Making Your Bulletin Boards Easy-to-Make and Easy-to-Do

Creating exciting bulletin boards can brighten up your entire library or classroom, calling attention to subjects you want to highlight. *Simply Incredible Bulletin Boards* includes a series of bulletin boards that honor the birthdays of some of the best-loved authors and illustrators of children's literature. You'll also find a series of bulletin boards that highlight exciting periods throughout history that will take your readers on fantastic journeys from flying though space to sailing the high seas. Have fun creating bulletin boards that are...*simply incredible!*

As you read through the suggestions here, keep in mind that each board is designed to work in a variety of situations. If your bulletin board proportions are different from the sample displays, use the tips offered in Design Basics starting on the next page to rearrange the pattern pieces for your setting. The general information below will help you start creating effective and dramatic bulletin boards that are easy and inexpensive to make.

Bulletin board themes & patterns
Bulletin board patterns
Patterns for the individual elements of each bulletin board are provided so that you can mix and match pieces to create displays that fit your setting. Each element can be enlarged using an opaque or overhead projector; or following the drawings in the book, you can create your own patterns freehand. The number of elements you choose will be determined by the amount of space you have and the amount of time you have to create them.

Kids can make it!
There are fun, theme-related crafts that correspond with each of the bulletin boards. Getting children involved is critical to creating memorable learning experiences and for motivating youngsters to read about each of the selected topics. Projects can be constructed as separate activities and then included as part of the bulletin board or displayed elsewhere around the room.

Bulletin boards that display children's work
Bulletin board designs can be altered to display various forms or styles of work completed by the children. For example, in the "Happy Birthday Jules Verne," children can write book reports or poems about their travels on balloons. These works can be arranged on the bulletin board in rows under a banner or hung around the room. With the "Dinosaur Days" bulletin board, children can make their own dinosaurs and arrange them on the prehistoric background.

Foldout table displays
You can share other materials on a topic which cannot be displayed on the bulletin board by creating a matching table display. Each theme includes some starter suggestions for books and items to display as well as ways to arrange these materials that will spark any child's imagination.

To create the table displays, you will need the following materials:

- ❖ poster board
- ❖ clear packing tape
- ❖ scissors
- ❖ pencil
- ❖ yardstick

You can make a table display to match your bulletin board by following these directions:

1. Cut a 22"x 28" sheet of poster board in half, lengthwise. Cut one of the halves of poster board in half, widthwise.

2. Lay poster board sections flat on a table with the long section in the middle and short sections on opposite ends. Using clear packing tape, tape the ends of the longer section to the short sections, creating a foldout display.

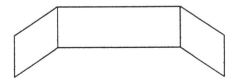

3. Staple or glue coordinating elements from the bulletin board to the table display.

4. To store, fold both sides inward.

Bookmarks

Children love to collect bookmarks, making them perfect for introducing a new subject, as well as reinforcing the joy of reading. In each chapter, there is a reproducible bookmark provided so you can give one to each of your eager readers.

Booklists for display suggestions

A book list is included with each chapter to assist you in your search for books which can be displayed.

Design basics

Composition

You want to create a composition that moves the viewer's eyes around the board and holds their interest. Each design provides a visual pathway for viewers to follow. The title, for instance, causes the eyes to move from left to right. From there, the eyes should move into and around the board. Before stapling elements in place, pin them up with straight pins. Stand across the room and look at your composition. Does your eye get stuck? If so, make some adjustments and staple in place.

Dividing the composition

When designing your composition, you want to divide the space so your viewer will want to keep exploring the picture. A symmetrical composition, where the divisions are equal, appears static and without movement.

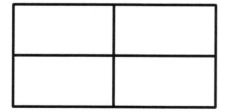

An asymmetrical composition, with unequal divisions, is more dynamic and causes the viewer to take a longer look at the composition.

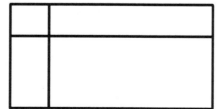

Movement and direction

One way to keep your viewer's eyes moving is to let them know where their eyes should go next. In this example, the viewer doesn't know where to look first, and your so their attention will wander aimlessly.

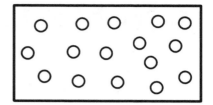

By placing the circles in a pattern with a definite direction, dramatic movement is created. Your viewer's attention has been grabbed and sent along a pathway.

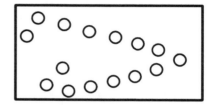

Figure-ground relationship

You can make a bulletin board that is easier for viewers to read by making it clear where the figure is in relationship to the background. This composition appears flat and the competing patterns makes it difficult to read. There is a lack of differentiation between the figure and background.

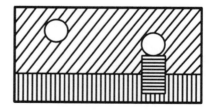

In this composition there is a greater contrast between figure and ground. There is more depth and the readability has been improved.

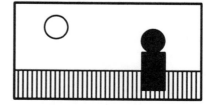

Creating a sense of depth will add interest to your bulletin board. In this example, the two identical squares make the picture look flat.

By varying the size of the squares, the larger one is made to look closer. A sense of depth has been created.

When the upper square overlaps the bottom one it appears that the upper one is on top.

In the last example, the black square moves back while the white square comes forward.

Colors

Each bulletin board design suggests a color scheme. These colors were chosen for several reasons:

❖ Colors are selected to be analogous (in the same family) and to blend together in the composition;

❖ Colors that contrast add interest and emphasis. For example, green and red are opposites on the color wheel and they are often used next to each other to add contrast;

❖ Colors that contrast with each other (dark and light), can be especially effective when creating text in an easy-to-read banner;

❖ Colors that are themed or connected with the subject. For example, red and green are associated with Christmas; pastels are theme colors for Easter.

Texture

Textures can add a lot to the design and impact of your boards, without adding a lot of expense. Use a variety of textures when selecting materials: colored tissue paper, aluminum foil, textured paint, corrugated paper and yarn.

Time savers

Here are a few time-saving tips:

1. Choose fewer elements to make your composition. For example, in the "Ancient Mythology" there is a banner and three gods. You can simplify this board by making the banner, Pegasus and stars.

2. Many hands make light work. Have a group of children help color and cut out the different elements of your bulletin board.

3. Make a bulletin board of children's work and you only need to make the background and banner.

4. When cutting patterns, stack papers and cut two to three items at the same time.

Storing bulletin boards to use again

Once you have created a beautiful bulletin board, you can store it—and save time next year!

1. Take a picture of each bulletin board. Store one set of photos in a picture file or photo album for further reference, and list the photos by title.

2. Remove the staples from the bulletin board. Then lay the flat elements on top of the background craft paper and roll the craft paper into a tube. Use a large rubber band to secure the tube. Now make a stronger storage container from an empty cardboard tube. (Ask a carpet store to save them for you.) You can cut carpet tubes down to size with a coping saw or a serrated knife. Make a cap for the bottom opening with masking tape to cover the hole or by gluing strips of paper across the opening. Write the title of the board on each tube.

3. To store thicker or three-dimensional elements or small loose pieces, create a storage portfolio for the objects by taking two sheets of poster board or cardboard that are the same size and tape them together on three sides. Label the outside of the portfolio.

Lewis Carroll

Bulletin board is based on characters from *Alice's Adventures in Wonderland*

Directions ▼   Patterns on p. 11

1. BACKGROUND: Staple yellow craft paper over the bulletin board background.

2. BANNER: Enlarge banner design (p. 9) onto white craft paper. Outline letters and design with black marker. Color in letters and border with black and red markers. Color Cheshire Cat with yellow and orange markers. Cut out banner and staple to bulletin board.

3. ROSE BUSHES: Enlarge bushes onto green craft paper. Outline with black marker and cut out. Staple bushes to board. Cut crepe paper into 15" pieces. Roll each piece of crepe paper onto itself. Pinch crepe paper at the bottom and flare out at the top as you go (See sample, p.10). Staple roses onto bushes.

4. FIGURES: Enlarge figures onto white craft paper and outline with black round-tip, felt marker. Using black, yellow, orange, red and bright blue markers, color in figures. Cut out figures and staple to bulletin board.

Supplies ▼

Materials you need

- bright yellow craft paper for the background
- white craft paper for the banner and figures
- green craft paper for the rose bushes
- black, red, yellow, orange and bright blue, wide-tip felt markers
- 1 red roll and 1 white roll of crepe paper
- white glue

Tools you need

- opaque or overhead projector
- photocopy machine
- scissors
- stapler
- pins

Lewis Carroll

Lewis Carroll (1932–1898) is the pen name of Charles Lutwidge Dodgson, an English author, mathematician, and logician, best known for the immortal fantasy *Alice's Adventures in Wonderland,* popularized as *Alice in Wonderland.*

He was born on January 27, 1832, in Daresbury, Cheshire, where his father was the vicar. Carroll was educated at Rugby and at Christ Church College, University of Oxford. In 1863, he was ordained deacon, but chose not to go on to the priesthood. Instead he began lecturing in mathematics as a senior student, and then stayed on to teach until he was in his late forties.

In 1865, Lewis Carroll published *Alice's Adventures in Wonderland.* Its sequel, *Through the Looking-Glass and What Alice Found There*, appeared in 1872. These were followed by additional fantasy works, including: *Phantasmagoria and Other Poems* (1869), *The Hunting of the Snark* (1876), and a novel, *Sylvie and Bruno* (2 vol., 1889-93). He died at Guildford, Surrey, on January 14, 1898 at the age of 65.

Always a friend of children, Carroll wrote thousands of letters to them, delightful flights of fantasy, many illustrated with little sketches. These letters have been collected and published as *The Letters of Lewis Carroll* (2 vol., 1979) by Morton N. Cohen and Roger L. Green.

The Alice stories were originally written in 1862 for Alice Liddell (d. 1934), a daughter of Henry George Liddell, dean of Christ Church College. The works were illustrated by the English cartoonist Sir John Tenniel and immediately became popular books for children. The names and sayings of the characters, such as the March Hare, the Mad Hatter, the Cheshire Cat, and the White Knight, have become part of our everyday speech.

Banner / Bookmark

Photocopy and enlarge for **banner**. See directions on p. 8 for color suggestions.
For **bookmark**, photocopy and allow students to color.

Foldout Table Display

Follow "Foldout Table Display" directions on p. 5–6, using bright yellow poster board. Staple card figures and a rose bush to display. Use large paper flowers, playing cards and copies of various illustrations from *Alice in Wonderland* to enhance display.

Display books, videos, audio tapes and/or CD-ROMs on works by Lewis Carroll.

Books by Lewis Carroll

Alice's Adventures in Wonderland

Alice in Wonderland

Through the Looking Glass and What Alice Found

The Hunting of Snark

The Walrus and the Carpenter and Other Remarkable Stories

Phantasmagoria and Other Poems

Sylvie and Bruno

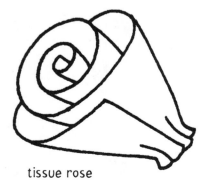

tissue rose

Kids Can Make It!

Photocopy "Wonderland" figures on p. 11 onto white construction paper. Have children color and cut out figures. Glue figures to craft sticks to make "Wonderland Puppets." Children can also make their own rose bushes using the bulletin board directions on p. 8.

Lewis Carroll
Wonderland patterns

Jules Verne

Bulletin board is based on images from *Around the World in Eighty Days*

Directions ▼   Patterns on p. 15

1. BACKGROUND: Cover bulletin board with bright blue craft paper.

2. BORDER: Cut white scalloped paper to fit the perimeter of bulletin board. Staple to board.

3. BALLOONS and BASKETS: Enlarge balloons and baskets onto white craft paper and outline with black marker. Color balloons, children and baskets with colored markers. Cut out balloons and baskets.

Fold large basket along dashed lines. Glue sides of basket together. Glue yarn onto back of balloons and then onto back of each basket. Staple balloons and baskets to bulletin board.

Supplies ▼

Materials you need

- bright blue craft paper for the background
- white craft paper for the balloons and baskets
- 1 roll white scalloped paper
- black, red, yellow, orange and hair and skin tone wide-tip felt markers
- black yarn
- white glue

Tools you need

- opaque or overhead projector
- photocopy machine
- scissors
- stapler
- pins

Jules Verne

Jules Verne (1828–1905) was born February 8, 1828, in Nantes, France. He went on to become one of the best known French authors of all time and is today regarded as the father of science fiction.

As a young man, Verne studied law in Paris, where he was also busy writing opera librettos and plays. In 1863, he published a short fantasy, "Five Weeks in a Balloon." This now famous story was rejected several times before one publisher suggested that Verne rewrite it as a "novel of imagination," or as we now know it, "science fiction." The final product, *Around the World in Eighty Days,* published in 1872, was an immediate success and encouraged Verne to continue his writing on science fiction themes.

Verne's keen interest in science and invention was a reflection of the time in which he lived. He knew a great deal about physics, mathematics and geography, voraciously reading the most current scientific papers of the day. Verne used this knowledge to make his fantasy stories more believable. He actually forecast with remarkable accuracy many scientific achievements of the twentieth century: flights into outer space, submarines, helicopters, air conditioning, guided missiles, and motion pictures long before they were developed. Verne also wrote several historical novels, including a story about the American Civil War, *North Against South* (1887).

Among his most popular books are *Journey to the Center of the Earth* (1864; trans. 1874), *From the Earth to the Moon* (1865; trans. 1873), *20,000 Leagues Under the Sea* (1870; trans. 1873), *Mysterious Island* (1870; trans. 1875), and *Around the World in Eighty Days* (1872; trans. 1873). Many are familiar with these works through the famous film retellings.

Bookmark

For **bookmark**, photocopy and allow students to color.

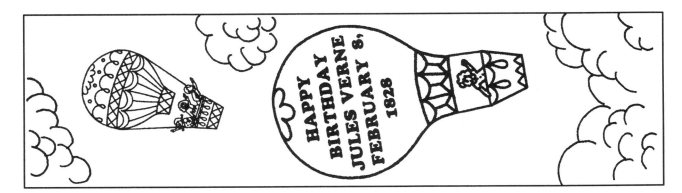

Foldout Table Display

Follow "Foldout Table Display" directions on p. 5–6, using bright blue poster board. Staple balloons, baskets and white scalloped paper to the display. Display miniatures of boats, trains, airplanes and submarines.

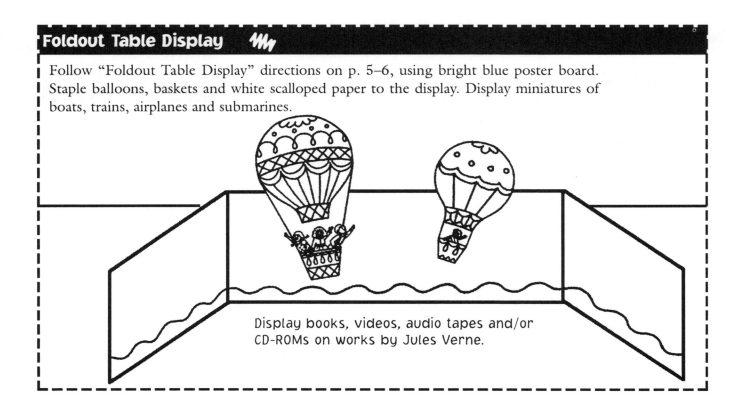

Display books, videos, audio tapes and/or CD-ROMs on works by Jules Verne.

Books by Jules Verne

Five Weeks in a Balloon

A Journey to the Center of the Earth

From the Earth to the Moon

Twenty Thousand Leagues Under the Sea

The Mysterious Island

Around the World in Eighty Days

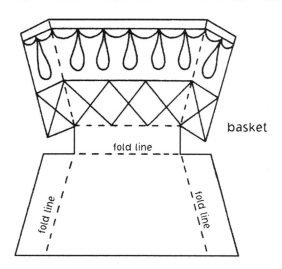

basket

fold line

fold line

fold line

Kids Can Make It!

Photocopy balloon and basket of children onto white construction paper. Have children make balloons by following step 3 of the directions on p. 12. Hang balloons from string around the room or staple to bulletin board.

balloon

Jules Verne balloon patterns

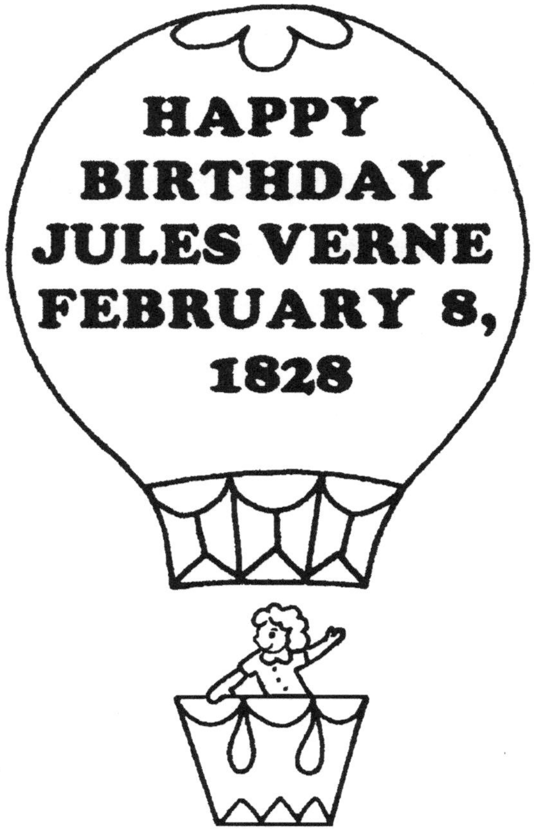
HAPPY
BIRTHDAY
JULES VERNE
FEBRUARY 8,
1828

Mitsumasa Anno

Bulletin board is based on *Anno's Math Games*

Directions ▼   Patterns on p. 19

1. BACKGROUND: Cover bulletin board with bright blue craft paper.

2. BANNER: Enlarge banner (p. 17) onto white craft paper and outline letters and design with black marker. Using markers, color title red, border pink, flowers yellow with red centers. Cut out banner and staple to bulletin board.

3. BORDER: Enlarge flower with five petals onto pink construction paper and outline with black marker. Color center of each flower red. Make one flower with only four petals. Cut out flowers and staple to board.

4. CAKES: Enlarge cake ① onto white craft paper ten times and outline with black marker. Enlarge cakes ② and ③ one time each and outline with black marker. Using pink, red and yellow markers to color cakes. Cut out cakes and staple to bulletin board.

5. CHILDREN: Enlarge children onto white craft paper and outline with black marker. Using markers, color hair any color, girl's dress yellow, boy's tie and pants red. Cut out children and staple to board.

Supplies ▼

Materials you need

- bright blue craft paper for the background
- white craft paper for the banner, children and cakes
- pink construction paper for the flowers
- black, red, yellow, pink, and hair color wide-tip, felt markers

Tools you need

- opaque or overhead projector
- photocopy machine
- scissors
- stapler
- pins

Mitsumasa Anno

Mitsumasa Anno, best known for his imaginative and thought-provoking picture books, is truly considered an "original" in the field of children's literature. Born on March 20, 1926, in the small town of Tsuwano in western Japan, Anno attributes his novel perspective to influences in his early years. His family owned a small inn, which served as the hub of a small farming community. Each week local farmers and cattle ranchers gathered together at his family's inn to sell their goods and share tales of family history and daily life.

As a child, Mitsumasa spent hours listening to their stories and drawing. He loved to sketch scenes from nature and recalls how he could find the forms or patterns in our everyday world. One day, a vagabond painter stayed at the inn, and Mitsumasa's father asked the artist to look at the boy's work. The painter was impressed but tried to tell the Anno's how difficult it would be to succeed as an artist. Fortunately, Mitsumasa was not discouraged.

Anno went to high school in a city far from his hometown where his commitment to art solidified. Unfortunately Anno could find little in the way of books or classes for artists in a Japan preparing for World War II. So he traveled to Paris, where he fell in love with the unique visions of Van Gough and Escher.

As World War II started, Anno was drafted into the Japanese army and returned to his homeland. It was a very difficult experience for him, one where he suffered more from beatings by the bullies in his own regiment than from injuries on the battlefield.

After the war, he could not forget the beatings. These experiences motivated Anno to write and illustrate his first picture book, *Topsy-Turvies*. He then wrote *Upside-Downers; Downside-Uppers* and *Magical Midnight Circus*.

Since then, Mitsumasa Anno has written many books and has become known world-wide as a creative thinker as well as illustrator. In 1984, Anno won the Hans Christian Andersen Prize, the highest honor attainable in the field of children's book illustration.

Banner / Bookmark

Photocopy and enlarge for **banner**. See directions on p. 16 for color suggestions.
For **bookmark**, photocopy onto bright blue, yellow or pink paper and allow students to color.

Follow "Fold Out Table Display" directions on p. 5–6, using bright blue poster board. Staple cakes that are all the same except for one to the display. Display puzzles and other visual games.

Display books, videos, audio tapes and/or CD-ROM's on works by Mitsumasa Anno; math concepts or numbers.

Books by Mitsumasa Anno

Topsy-Turvy: Pictures to Stretch the Imagination

Upside-Downers; Downside-Uppers: More Pictures to Stretch the Imagination

Dr. Anno's Magical Midnight Circus

Anno's Alphabet: An Adventure in Imagination

Anno's Counting Book

All in a Day

Anno's Britain

Anno's Counting House

Anno's Flea Market

Anno's Hat Tricks

Anno's Journey

Anno's Mysterious Multiplying Jar

Anno's U.S.A.

Socrates and the Three Little Pigs

Anno's Peekaboo

Anno's Faces

Anno's Math Games

Anno's Math Games II

Anno's Math Games III

Anno's Sundial

Anno's Masks

Anno's Twice Told Tales

Kids Can Make It!

Photocopy and enlarge bulletin board illustration from p.16 onto white 8½" x 11" paper. Have children find which cake has only six candles, which cake is missing a flower and which flower along the border only has four petals. Try other visual games such as making tangram puzzles.

Hans Christian Andersen

Happy Birthday
Hans Christian Andersen
April 2, 1805

Bulletin board is based on *The Little Mermaid*

Directions ▼   Patterns on p. 23

1. BACKGROUND: Cover bulletin board by cutting bright blue craft paper to the same size and stapling to board.

2. BANNER: Enlarge banner onto yellow craft paper. Outline and color in letters with bright blue marker. Cut out banner and staple to bulletin board.

3. MERMAID AND FISH: Enlarge mermaid (except for hair and scales) and fish onto white craft paper and outline with black marker. Using light green, bright blue, light purple and skin tone markers, color mermaid. Using orange and yellow markers, color fish. Cut out mermaid and fish. Trace scale pattern onto stack of tissue paper and cut out scales. Glue scales onto tail of mermaid and yarn onto her head for hair. Staple mermaid and fish onto board.

4. SEAWEED: Twist long pieces of green crepe paper and staple onto board.

Supplies ▼

Materials you need

- bright blue craft paper for the background
- bright yellow craft paper for the banner
- white craft paper for the mermaid and fish
- black, light green, bright blue, light purple, yellow, orange and skin tone, wide-tip, felt markers
- green, blue and light purple tissue paper for the scales
- yellow, orange, brown or black yarn for the hair
- 1 roll of green crepe paper for seaweed
- white glue

Tools you need

- opaque or overhead projector
- photocopy machine
- scissors
- stapler
- pins

Hans Christian Andersen

Something About the Author

Hans Christian Andersen (1805–1875) was born on April 2, 1805, in Odense, Denmark. He created the literary background for the Danish culture from stories told to him by family members, neighbors and friends.

Although Andersen wrote in many genres, including plays, novels, poetry and travel books, he is mostly known for his fairy tales. Unlike most fairy tales, many of Andersen's stories do not end happily. His themes are often moralistic—even religious—urging readers to look at their own behavior in daily life. And while some stories take a lighthearted and humorous look at human foibles, Andersen was quite serious in his desire to eliminate hypocrisy, mistrust, lying, and cheating in daily life.

Andersen's childhood was one of poverty and neglect. At the age of fourteen, he ran away to Copenhagen, where he became an apprentice at the Royal Theater. Patrons who noticed him there provided for his education. His first real success began with his first novel, *The Improvisatore, or Life in Italy* (1835; trans. 1845). This work was well received by the critics, and soon after, he published a collection of four of his fairy tales.

Andersen later traveled throughout Europe, Asia, and Africa, writing many plays, novels, and travel books. He continued to write fairy tales, often inspired by children he met along the way. His more than 150 stories for children have established him as one of the most widely read authors in history. Among his most famous tales of fantasy are "The Ugly Duckling," "The Emperor's New Clothes," "The Snow Queen," "The Brave Tin Soldier," "The Red Shoes," and "The Little Mermaid." These stories and others have been translated into more than 80 languages and have been the source of plays, ballets, films, and works of sculpture and painting.

Banner / Bookmark

Photocopy and enlarge for **banner**. See directions on p. 20 for color suggestions.
For **bookmark**, photocopy onto bright blue or green paper and allow students to color.

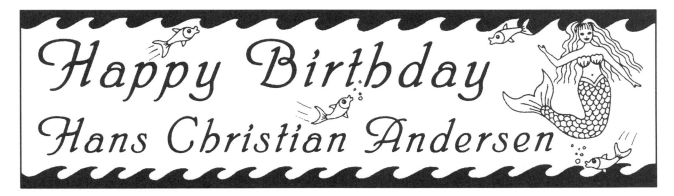

Foldout Table Display

Follow "Fold Out Table Display" directions on p. 5–6, using bright blue poster board. Cut waves along the top of display. Enlarge mermaid and fish onto white poster board and outline with black, wide-tip felt marker. Follow the directions in step 3 on p. 20 to complete mermaid and fish. Cut out figures and staple to display. Use photos or figures of mermaids and ships. Add sea shells and fish netting to display.

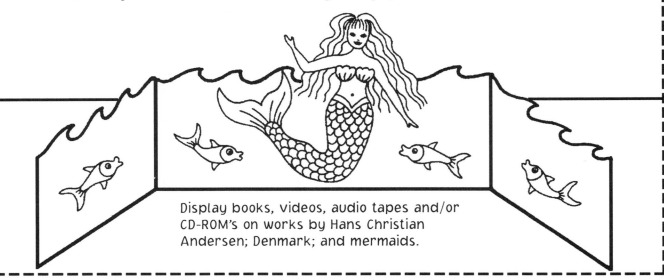

Display books, videos, audio tapes and/or CD-ROM's on works by Hans Christian Andersen; Denmark; and mermaids.

Some Stories by H C Andersen

Thumbelina
The Brave Tin Soldier
The Ugly Duckling
The Snow Queen
The Little Mermaid
Little Claus and Big Claus
The Metal Pig
The Nightingale
The Marsh King's Daughter
The Elfin Hill
The Shadow
The Story of the Wind
The Emperor's New Suit
The Princess and the Pea
The Red Shoes
The Wicked Prince
The Little Match Girl

Kids Can Make It!

Photocopy mermaid on p. 23 onto white construction paper. Have children color and cut out mermaids. Glue yarn onto mermaids to make hair. Glue mermaids to craft sticks to make "Mermaid Puppets." Make a puppet show, display mermaids on bulletin board or make mobiles with mermaids and fish.

Hans Christian Andersen mermaid patterns

scale pattern

Sir Arthur Conan Doyle

Directions ▼

Patterns on p. 27

1. BACKGROUND: Cover bulletin board by cutting green craft paper to the same size and stapling to board.

2. BANNER: Enlarge banner (p. 25) design onto white craft paper. Outline letters and design with black marker. Color in letters and border with black, green and red markers. Cut out banner and staple to bulletin board.

3. FIGURES: Enlarge figures onto white craft paper and outline with black marker. Using markers color in designs. Cut out figures and staple to bulletin board.

4. SHOE PRINTS: Enlarge shoe print onto black craft paper and outline with a white pencil. Cut out shoe prints and staple to the board.

Supplies ▼

Materials you need

- green craft paper for the background
- white craft paper for the banner and figures
- black craft paper for shoe prints
- black, brown, red, yellow, orange, green and hair and skin wide-tip, felt markers
- white pencil

Tools you need

- opaque or overhead projector
- photocopy machine
- scissors
- stapler
- pins

Sir Arthur Conan Doyle

Something About the Author

Arthur Conan Doyle (1859–1930) was born on May 22, 1859, in Edinburgh and educated at Stonyhurst College and the University of Edinburgh. He became a physician and practiced medicine in Southsea, England, for eight years from 1882 to 1890.

During these years he began writing short stories and novellas. The first of 68 stories, "A Study in Scarlet," appeared in 1887, featuring his most unforgettable character—Sherlock Holmes. Holmes' ingenious deductive reasoning was based on Doyle's training as a physician and one of the author's own university professors. Conan Doyle was immediately successful in his literary career, so successful that within five years he had abandoned his medical practice to devote his entire time to writing.

Some of the best known of the Holmes stories are "The Sign of Four" (1890), "The Adventures of Sherlock Holmes" (1892), "The Hound of the Baskervilles" (1902), and "His Last Bow" (1917). These works made Conan Doyle internationally famous and popularized the detective-story genre. Conan Doyle also wrote historical romances, such as *Micah Clarke* (1888), *The White Company* (1890), *Rodney Stone* (1896), and *Sir Nigel* (1906), and a play *A Story of Waterloo* (1894).

In 1900, after serving in the Boer War as a physician, Conan Doyle wrote *The Great Boer War* and *The War in South Africa: Its Causes and Conduct* (1902), in which he promoted England's participation in the conflict as justified. For these works, Doyle was knighted in 1902. After the death of his eldest son in World War I, Sir Arthur became an advocate of spiritualism, lecturing and writing extensively on the subject. His autobiography, *Memories and Adventures*, was published in 1924, six years before his death.

Banner / Bookmark

Photocopy and enlarge for **banner**. See directions on p. 24 for color suggestions.
For **bookmark**, photocopy onto tan, red or green paper and allow students to color.

Foldout Table Display

Follow "Foldout Table Display" directions on p. 5–6, using green poster board. Staple figures and shoe prints to display.

Display books, videos, audio tapes and/or CD-ROM's on works by Sir Arthur Conan Doyle.

Some Sherlock Holmes stories

Collections of stories:
The Adventures of Sherlock Holmes
The Memoirs of Sherlock Homes
The Return of Sherlock Homes

Sherlock Holmes Stories Retold for Children
Mysteries of Sherlock Holmes. Judith Conaway, 1994.
The Adventure of the Dancing Men. Murray Shaw, 1993.
Mystery! Mystery! (sound recording) Jim Weiss, 1993.
The Adventure of Abbey Grange. Murray Shaw, 1991.
Sherlock Holmes for Children (sound recording) Jim Weiss, 1991.
The Adventure of the Speckled Band. Murray Shaw, 1991.
The Adventure of the Copper Beeches. Murray Shaw, 1990.
The Adventure of the Cardboard Box. Murray Shaw, 1990.
The Adventure of Black Peter. Murray Shaw, 1990.
Match Wits with Sherlock Holmes. Murray Shaw, 1990.

Kids Can Make It!

Have children write secrete messages to each other and decode them. Write the alphabet on one line, then write it again on the line directly below the first one, but start with the letter B instead of A.

ABCDEFGHIJKLMNOPQRSTUVWXYZ

BCDEFGHIJKLMNOPQRSTUVWXYZA

To encode a message, find each letter of the message in the top line and match it with the corresponding letter in the code line. Using the system above, for example the word "cat" becomes "dbu."

Nz gbwpsjuf dpmps jt cmvf. Xibu't zpvs't?

My favorite color is blue. What's your's?

Sir Arthur Conan Doyle
detective patterns

Charlotte Zolotow

Happy Birthday
Charlotte Zolotow
June 26, 1915

Directions ▼ Patterns on p. 31

1. BACKGROUND: Cover top third of bulletin board with light blue craft paper. Staple light blue craft paper to board. Cover bottom two thirds of board by cutting green craft paper the same width as board. Staple green craft paper to board.

2. TITLE: Enlarge title onto bulletin board and outline and fill in title with black marker.

3. CHILDREN: Enlarge children onto white craft paper and outline with black marker. Color children's clothing with darker colors such as red, purple or blue markers. Cut out and staple to board.

4. FLOWERS: Enlarge flowers to 4" in diameter and outline onto yellow construction paper. Cut out flowers and curl petals upward with your fingers or a pencil. Cut orange tissue paper into 4" squares. Crumple each square of tissue paper into a ball and glue each ball to the center of a flower. Staple flowers to bulletin board.

Supplies ▼

Materials you need

- light blue craft paper for the sky
- green craft paper for the grass
- white craft paper for the children
- yellow construction paper for the flowers
- orange tissue paper or crepe paper for centers of flowers
- black, green, bright blue, orange, purple, red and hair and skin tone wide-tip, felt markers
- white glue

Tools you need

- opaque or overhead projector
- photocopy machine
- scissors
- stapler
- pins

Charlotte Zolotow

Something About the Author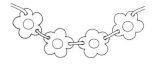

Charlotte Zolotow was born in 1915 in Norfolk, Virginia. She had learned to read before she went to school. When asked what she wanted to do when she grew up, Charlotte always said she wanted to write books and draw the pictures for them.

Zolotow attended the University of Wisconsin on a writing scholarship. While in college, she focused on her writing skills and did not study art at all. She married Maurice Zolotow, whom she met at the University, and after graduation began working at Harper's Children's Books as an assistant editor.

While at Harper's she proposed a book idea to her editor, Ursula Nordstrom, who encouraged her to write the work herself. The result, *The Park Book*, was completed just before the birth of her son, Stephen. Later books were inspired by bedtime stories and day-to-day experiences with her son.

Her daughter, Ellen, born eight years later, served as another source of inspiration for additional children's stories. Zolotow captures the unique perspective of youngsters and their fresh view of the universe.

Happy Birthday Charlotte Zolotow bookmark

Photocopy bookmark onto yellow, pink, orange or green, copier paper.

Foldout Table Display

Follow "Foldout Table Display" directions on p. 5–6, using green poster board. Staple children and flowers to the display. Add pots or vases of fresh flowers to display.

Display books, videos, audio tapes and/or CD-ROM's on works by Charlotte Zolotow.

Selected books by C. Zolotow

Peter and the Pigeons
Snippets: A Gathering of Poems and Pictures
This Quiet Lady
The Seashore Book
The Summer Night
Something Is Going to Happen
The Quiet Mother and the Noisy Little Boy
Not a Little Monkey
Sleepy Book
A Tiger Called Thomas
The Poodle Who Barked at the Wind
I Like to Be Little
Over and Over
Timothy Too
Summer Is
Some Things Go Together
But Not Billy
The White Marble
The Big Brother
The New Friend
If You Listen
Say It
River Winding
Some New
My Grandson
My Grandson Lew
Janey
William's Doll
A Father Like That
Wake Up and Good Night
The Hating Book
The Quarreling Book
Mr. Rabbit and the Lovely Present

Kids Can Make It!

Trace six or more flowers onto 8½" x 11" sheet of white paper. Outline flowers with black, round-tip felt marker and photocopy onto white construction paper. Have children color and cut out flowers. Punch holes in flowers and string onto green yarn to make flower necklaces. Children can also make flowers following the directions in step 4 on p. 28 and tape drinking straws to the back of them.

flower pattern

flower necklace

Charlotte Zolotow patterns

sample flower with tissue center

Beatrix Potter

Happy Birthday
Beatrix Potter
July 6, 1866

Bulletin board is based on *The Tale of Peter Rabbit*

Directions ▼ Patterns on p. 35

1. SKY: Cover top half of bulletin board with yellow craft paper.

2. DIRT: Cut out 12" strips of brown craft paper, the same width as the board. Cut a wavy pattern across the top of each strip. Staple strips in an overlapping pattern onto bottom third of board.

3. TITLE: Enlarge title onto board and outline and fill in with green, wide-tip felt marker.

4. RABBIT and WATERING CAN: Enlarge rabbit onto white craft paper and watering can onto green poster board. Outline designs in black marker. Color rabbit with light brown marker. Cut out rabbit and watering can. Cut watering can along dotted lines with craft knife. Insert spout and handle into watering can and tape in place. Fold tabs under and staple watering can to bulletin board. Place rabbit inside watering can and staple rabbit to board.

5. CARROTS: Enlarge carrot onto orange construction paper and leaves onto green construction paper, then outline with black marker. Cut out carrots and leaves. Glue leaves onto carrots. Insert carrots into dirt and staple in place.

Supplies ▼

Materials you need
- yellow craft paper for the sky
- brown craft paper for dirt
- green poster board for the watering can
- white craft paper for the rabbit
- green & orange construction paper for carrots
- pencil
- black, light brown & green wide-tip, felt markers
- transparent tape

Tools you need
- photocopy machine
- scissors
- stapler
- pins
- craft knife

Beatrix Potter

(Helen) Beatrix Potter (1866-1943) was an English writer and illustrator of children's books. She was born on July 6, 1866, in London, and educated in private schools. During most of her adult life, Beatrix Potter lived in a farm cottage in Sawrey, Westmoreland County, where she kept many animals as pets.

Potter's first attempts to publish her illustrations (watercolors of fungi) were unsuccessful. And so she wrote and self-published a story about a family of animal characters as she entertained a friend's child who was an invalid. This story, *The Tale of Peter Rabbit* (1900), became a children's classic throughout the world.

Other animal characters created by Potter in this series include Benjamin Bunny, Jemima Puddle-Duck, and Mrs. Tiggy-Winkle. Inseparable from her whimsical tales are her delicate and detailed watercolor illustrations, depicting her characters in domestic scenes. Potter's other works include *The Tailor of Gloucester* (1902) and *The Tale of Tom Kitten* (1907).

Upon her death, Beatrix Potter bequeathed her property in Sawrey to the National Trust, which also maintains her home as a museum to preserve the natural landscape of her homeland.

Happy Birthday Beatrix Potter bookmark

Photocopy bookmark onto green, blue, yellow or light brown copier paper.

Foldout Table Display

Follow "Foldout Table Display" directions on p. 5–6, using light blue poster board. Staple brown craft paper, rabbit, watering can and carrots to display. Add stuffed animals or figures from Beatrix Potter's books, potted plants and baskets to display.

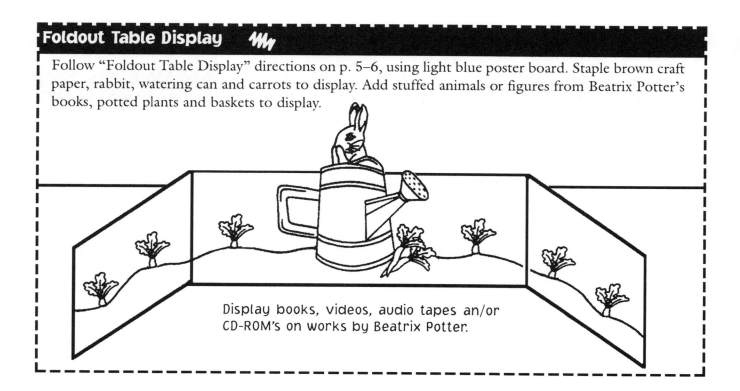

Display books, videos, audio tapes an/or CD-ROM's on works by Beatrix Potter.

Books by Beatrix Potter

The Tale of Squirrel Nutkin
The Tale of Tom Kitten
The Tale of Benjamin Bunny
The Tale of Jemima Puddle-Duck
The Tale of Peter Rabbit
The Taylor of Gloucester
The Tale of Mrs. Tiggy-Winkle
The Tale of Pigling Bland
The Tale of Miss Moppet
The Tale of Two Bad Mice
What Time Is It Peter Rabbit?
The Tale of Samuel Whiskers
The Tale of Little Pig Robinson
The Tale of Mrs. Tittlemouse
The Tale of Mr. Tod
The Tale of a Fierce Bad Rabbit
The Tale of Ginger and Pickles
The Tale of the Pie and the Patty-Pan
The Tale of Flopsy Bunnies
The Tale of Tuppenny
The Fairy Caravan

Kids Can Make It!

Photocopy watering can and rabbit on p. 35 onto white construction paper. Have children color and cut out rabbit and can. Cut along dotted lines with scissors then insert handle and spout into can. Glue can around a 6 oz. paper cup. Glue rabbit to a craft stick. Poke a hole in bottom of cup and insert craft stick. Slide stick up and down to make rabbit pop up and down.

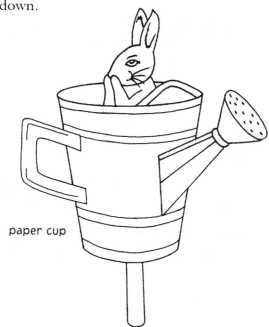

paper cup

watering can

handle

spout

carrots

Ray Bradbury

Bulletin board is based on *The Illustrated Man*

Directions ▼   Patterns on p. 39

1. BACKGROUND: Cover bulletin board by cutting bright blue craft paper to the same size and stapling to board.

2. ILLUSTRATED MAN: Enlarge Illustrated Man onto white craft paper and outline with black marker. Color illustrations with brightly-colored markers. Cut out Illustrated Man and staple to board.

3. BORDER: Cut orange scalloped paper to fit the perimeter of bulletin board. Staple to board.

4. TITLE and SUN: Enlarge title onto a large circle of yellow craft paper. Outline and fill in letters with red marker. Cut out yellow circle and staple to board.

Supplies ▼

Materials you need

- bright blue craft paper for the background
- bright yellow craft paper for the sun and title
- white craft paper for the Illustrated Man
- 1 roll orange scalloped paper
- black, red, blue, green, orange, yellow and purple wide-tip, felt markers

Tools you need

- opaque or overhead projector
- photocopy machine
- scissors
- stapler
- pins

Ray Bradbury

Something About the Author

Ray Bradbury was born on August 22, 1920, in Waukegan, Illinois. He comes from a long line of editors and publishers, who at one time owned a Chicago-based publishing company, Bradbury & Sons. Bradbury's style is considered one of this century's most unique—somewhere between science fiction and fantasy. His tales of science fiction have less to do with science than with those who abuse science; his tales of fantasy have less to do with bizarre events than the inner workings of the human mind.

Ray Bradbury began sending his stories to magazines while still in high school. From 1941 to 1945, he sold "sci-fi" and detective stories to smaller magazines, selling his first major short story, "The Big Black and White Game," to the *American Mercury* in 1945. This story later appeared in *The Best American Short Stories of 1946*, edited by Martha Foley.

Ray Bradbury's first book of short stories, *Dark Carnivals*, was published in 1946. The well-known *Martian Chronicles* (1950) and *Dandelion Wine* (1957) were novels that centered about the strange events of a single geographical location. *Fahrenheit 451*, a short novel, focused more on themes of human interaction. Many of Bradbury's works have been adapted to films, owing mainly to the visual impact of his works.

Bradbury has not just confined himself to tales of the fantastic. He has written many realistic stories about the plight of Mexicans, Irishmen and Chicanos—stories about people who have found themselves disinherited or disoriented in 20th century mainstream America. Whether Bradbury is writing about "Green Town, Illinois," or the vast hostile landscape of Mars, beneath every setting is a small town lost in the midst of isolation. The lesson of his works is not the destruction of an alienated spirit but the optimism for what lies ahead. In short, Ray Bradbury writes to integrate positive human values into action.

Happy Birthday Ray Bradbury bookmark

Photocopy bookmark onto white, yellow or orange copier paper. Have children color as desired.

Foldout Table Display

Follow "Foldout Table Display" directions on p. 5–6, using bright blue poster board. Staple Illustrated Man to the display.

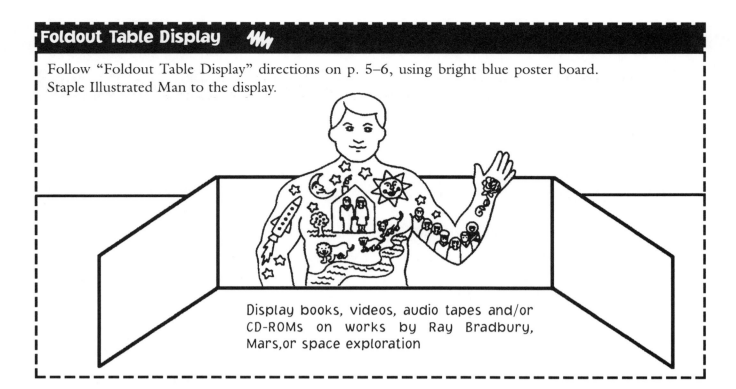

Display books, videos, audio tapes and/or CD-ROMs on works by Ray Bradbury, Mars, or space exploration

Books by Ray Bradbury

The Toynbee Convector
Death Is a Lonely Business
Something Wicked This Way Comes
The Haunted Computer and the Android Pope
The Stories of Ray Bradbury
Where Robot Mice and Robot men Run Round in Robot Towns
Long After Midnight
Dandelion Wine
When Elephants Last in the Dooryard Bloomed
The Halloween Tree
The October Country
I Sing the Body Electric!
Switch on the Night
The Illustrated Man
The Martian Chronicles
R Is for Rocket
Dark Carnival
The Machineries of Joy
The Anthem Sprinters
A Medicine for Melancholy
Fahrenheit 451
Golden Apples of the Sun

Kids Can Make It!

Trace outline of Illustrated Man on p. 39 onto an 8½"x11" sheet of white paper and outline with black, round-tip felt marker. Photocopy outline of man onto white construction paper. Have children illustrate their own stories on the inside of the man. Display illustrations on bulletin board or around the room.

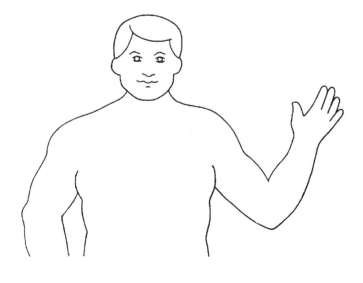

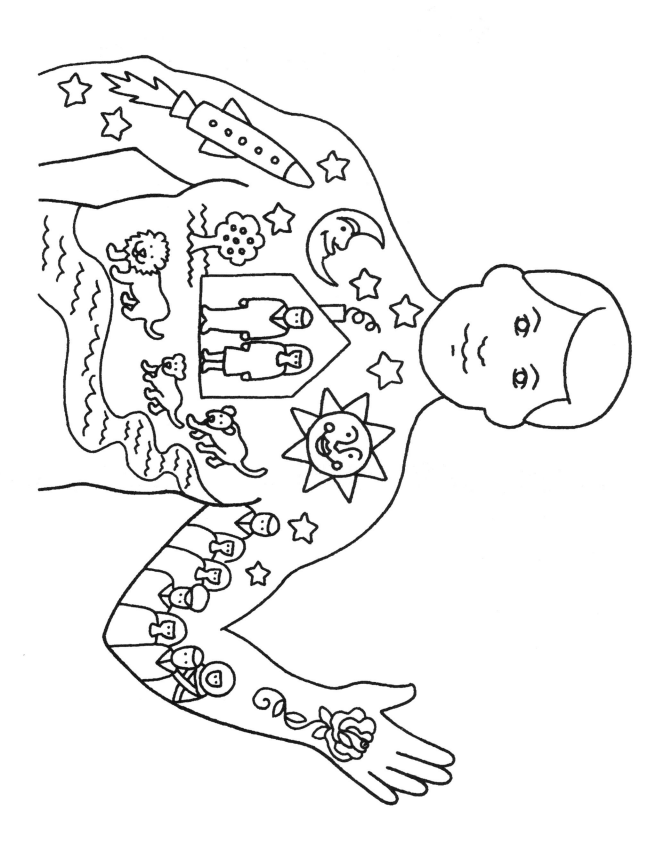

Roald Dahl

Happy
Birthday
Roald Dahl
September 13,
1916

Bulletin board is based on characters from *James and the Giant Peach*

Directions ▼   Patterns on p. 43

1. BACKGROUND: Cover bulletin board with light blue craft paper.

2. WAVES: Cover bottom section of board with dark blue craft paper. Cut a wave pattern across the top of dark blue paper. Staple to bottom of the board.

3. PEACH and TITLE: Enlarge peach onto orange craft paper and outline peach and title with black marker. Shade peach with pink and yellow pastel chalks. Color stem with brown marker. Cut out peach and staple to board.

4. BIRDS: Enlarge birds onto white craft paper and outline with black marker. Cut out birds and along dotted lines on body. Fold birds in half and slip wings through slits. Fold wings of bird up. (Sample on p. 42.) Staple birds to board. Tie white yarn around birds necks and glue ends of yarn to stem of peach.

5. BOY and SHARKS: Enlarge boy and sharks onto white craft paper and outline with black marker. Color the shark gray. Color boy using hair and skin tone markers and white, red and blue for his clothes. Cut out boy and sharks, then staple to bulletin board.

Supplies ▼

Materials you need

- light blue craft paper for the background
- dark blue craft paper for the water
- orange craft paper for the peach
- white craft paper for the birds, sharks and boy
- black, brown, gray, red, blue, hair and skin tone wide-tip, felt markers
- pink and yellow pastel chalks
- white yarn
- white glue

Tools you need

- opaque or overhead projector
- photocopy machine
- scissors
- stapler
- pins

Roald Dahl

Roald Dahl was born on September 13, 1916, in Llandaff, South Wales, to a family of five sisters and one brother. His father died when Roald was four and at the age of seven, Roald was sent to Repton, a highly-respected boarding school.

At eighteen, Roald turned down an offer to attend Oxford and instead joined the staff of the Shell Oil Company. At twenty, Shell Oil sent him to Tanzania, where he remained until the beginning of World War II. He then enlisted in the Royal Air Force, and in 1940, while fighting over the western desert of Libya, he was shot down. Dahl spent six months in the hospital and then rejoined his squadron in Greece. However, his injuries eventually forced him to return to England.

In 1942, Dahl was sent to Washington, DC as part of the British Air Attaché. During this time he began writing stories. His first children's story was called "The Gremlins" (1943). Dahl married actress Patricia Neal and together they have five children. His children inspired him to write *James and the Giant Peach* (1960); *Charlie and the Chocolate Factory* (1964); and the *Magic Finger* (1966). Dahl also wrote three short stories for adults: "Over to You," "Someone Like You" and "Kiss Kiss." He has twice won the Edgar Allan Poe Award and three of his works have become successful feature films: *James and the Giant Peach, Willie Wonka and the Chocolate Factory* and *The Gremlins*.

Happy Birthday Roald Dahl bookmark

Photocopy bookmark onto orange, or blue copier paper. Or copy onto plain paper and have children color.

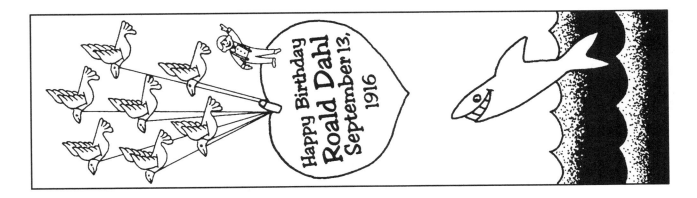

Foldout Table Display

Follow "Foldout Table Display" directions on p. 5–6 using light blue poster board. Staple peach, waves, shark and boy to the display.

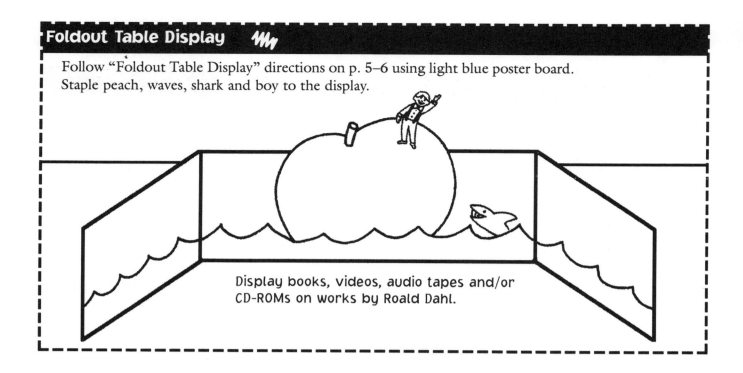

Display books, videos, audio tapes and/or CD-ROMs on works by Roald Dahl.

Books by Roald Dahl

James and the Giant Peach
Charlie and the Chocolate Factory
Willie Wonka and the Chocolate Factory
Matilda
The Magic Finger
Roald Dahl's Revolting Rhymes
Roald Dahl's Revolting Recipes
My Year
The Witches
Charlie and the Glass Elevator
The Vicar of Nibbleswicke
The Mimpins
The Twits
Rhyme Stew
Fantastic Mr. Fox
The Giraffe, and the Pelly and Me
Dirty Beasts
The BFG

Kids Can Make It!

Photocopy bird pattern and wings on p. 43 onto white construction paper. Have children make birds according to directions on p. 40. Hang birds from strings around the room or staple to bulletin board.

bird pattern

wings

Lois Lenski

HAPPY BIRTHDAY
LOIS LENSKI
OCTOBER 14, 1893

Bulletin board is based on *The Strawberry Girl*

Directions ▼   Patterns on p. 47

1. BACKGROUND: Cover bulletin board by cutting yellow craft paper to the same size and stapling to board. Cover bottom third of bulletin board by cutting brown craft paper the same width as bulletin board. Cut top of brown craft paper to look like a wavy line. Staple to bulletin board.

2. BORDER: Cut green scalloped paper to fit the perimeter of bulletin board. Staple to board.

3. TITLE: Enlarge title onto bulletin board and outline and fill in "Happy Birthday Lois Lenski" with red marker and "October 14, 1893" with green marker.

4. GIRL and BASKETS: Enlarge girl and baskets onto white craft paper and outline with black marker. Color bonnet blue with a red bow, dress with blue and white checks, strawberries red and green and baskets tan. Cut out girl and baskets. Fold baskets along dashed lines. Glue sides of baskets together. Staple girl and baskets to bulletin board.

Supplies ▼

Materials you need

- yellow craft paper for the background
- brown craft paper for the dirt
- white craft paper for the girl and baskets
- 1 roll green scalloped paper
- black, red, blue, green, tan, hair and skin tone wide-tip, felt markers
- white glue

Tools you need

- opaque or overhead projector
- photocopy machine
- scissors
- stapler
- pins

Lois Lenski

Lois Lenski was born in Springfield, Ohio, on October 14, 1893. The daughter of a Lutheran minister, Lois was six when her parents moved with their five children to a small village, Anna, Ohio. There she spent her childhood in the country, and it was a lifestyle she would always love.

In 1911, she moved to Columbus, where her father became professor and later dean of the Theological Seminary. Lois graduated from Ohio State University College of Education, in 1915, expecting to teach. But one of her teachers in the art department suggested she travel to New York to study art for a year.

For four years Lenski worked at the Art Students League. She went to London for a year, where she studied with Walter Bayes at the Westminster School. There she illustrated three books. With this experience, Lenski soon found openings with American publishers. In 1927, she had her first exhibition in New York. In 1921 she had married Arthur Covey, the well-known mural painter. They moved to Connecticut and lived in an old colonial farmhouse. For a number of years, Lenski illustrated books by other authors, always trying to adhere closely to the period, mood, and atmosphere suggested by each book.

Writing her own books developed gradually. It began with two stories of her Ohio childhood, *Skipping Village* and *A Little Girl of 1900*. Lenski's picture books were inspired by the interests and needs of her son, Stephen. These were later followed by seven books based on careful research of American history. In all of her works, Lois Lenski attempts to bring the dignity and value of traditional American life to modern child readers.

Happy Birthday Lois Lenski bookmark

Photocopy bookmark onto yellow, green, red or blue copier paper.

Foldout Table Display

Follow "Foldout Table Display" directions on p. 5–6, using yellow poster board. Staple girl, baskets and brown craft paper to the display. Add checkered table cloth, baskets, artificial strawberries and antiques farm items to display.

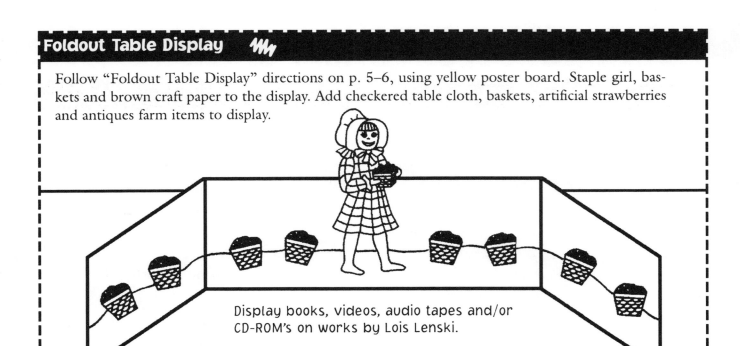

Display books, videos, audio tapes and/or CD-ROM's on works by Lois Lenski.

Selected books written or illustrated by Lois Lenski

Strawberry Girl
Little Sioux Girl
Berries in the Scoop
We Live By the River
Project Boy
Peanuts for Billy Ben
We live in the South
Coal Camp Girl
Houseboat Girl
Flood Friday
San Francisco Boy
Corn-Farm Boy
Mama Hattie's Girl
Prairie School
Texas Tomboy
Cotton in My Sack
Boom Town Boy
Judy's Journey
Blue Ridge Billy
Puritan Adventure
Bayou Suzette
Indian Captive
Blueberry Corners
Ocean Bon Mary
Bound Girl of Cobbie Hill

Kids Can Make It!

Photocopy strawberries on p. 47 onto white construction paper. Have children color and cut out strawberries. Punch holes in strawberries and string onto green yarn to make necklaces. Children can also make strawberry baskets and use them to hold book reports or cards on the bulletin board.

fold lines

fold lines

Fold baskets along dashed lines.
Glue sides of baskets together.

Mark Twain

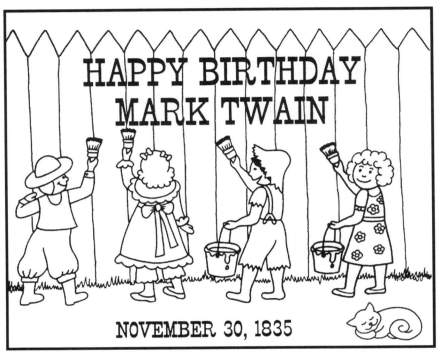

Bulletin board is based on characters from *The Adventures of Tom Sawyer*

Directions ▼   Patterns on p. 51

1. BACKGROUND: Cover bulletin board with white craft paper.

2. SKY: Cover top section of board with bright blue craft paper the same width as board. Cut a zigzag pattern across the top of bright blue paper. Staple to top of bulletin board.

3. FENCE and TITLE: Draw fence lines with brown marker. Enlarge title onto fence, then outline and fill in title with black marker.

4. GRASS: Cover bottom section of board with green craft paper the same width as board. Cut top of green paper to look like blades of grass. Staple to bottom of bulletin board.

5. CHILDREN and CAT: Enlarge children and cat onto white craft paper and outline with black marker. Using markers color figures. Cut out figures and staple to board.

Supplies ▼

Materials you need

- white craft paper for the background, children and cat
- bright blue craft paper for the sky
- green craft paper for the grass
- black, brown, yellow, red, blue, hair and skin tone wide-tip, felt markers

Tools you need

- opaque or overhead projector
- photocopy machine
- scissors
- stapler
- pins

Mark Twain

Mark Twain (1835–1910), American writer and humorist was born Samuel Clemens on November 30, 1835. His family moved to Hannibal, Missouri, when he was four years old, and it was this Mississippi river port that provided a rich background for his best-known works.

Clemens began his career in journalism as an apprentice to two Hannibal printers. In 1851 he began setting type and contributing sketches to his brother's newspaper, *The Hannibal Journal.* In 1861, he served briefly as a volunteer soldier in an irregular company of Confederate cavalry. Later that year, he accompanied his brother to the newly-created Nevada Territory, where he tried his hand at silver mining. In 1862, he became a reporter on the *Territorial Enterprise* in Virginia City, Nevada; and in 1863, Clemens began signing his articles with the now famous pseudonym. ("Mark Twain" is a Mississippi River phrase meaning "two fathoms deep." It was a measurement taken to make sure the water was deep enough for passage.)

After moving to San Francisco in 1864, Twain met writers Artemus Ward and Bret Harte, who encouraged him to write his own stories in his own style. In 1865, Twain reworked a tale he had heard in the California gold fields. Within months the short story, "The Celebrated Jumping Frog of Calaveras County," had become a national sensation.

Much of Twain's best work was written in the 1870s and '80s: *Roughing It* (1872) recounts his early adventures as a miner and journalist; *The Adventures of Tom Sawyer* (1876) celebrates boyhood in a town on the Mississippi River. *A Tramp Abroad* (1880) describes a walking trip through the Black Forest of Germany and the Swiss Alps. *The Prince and the Pauper* (1882), a children's book, focuses on switched identities in Tudor England; *Life on the Mississippi* (1883) combines an autobiographical account of his experiences as a river pilot with a visit to the Mississippi nearly two decades after he left it. *The Adventures of Huckleberry Finn* (1884), the sequel to Tom Sawyer, is considered Twain's masterpiece.

Happy Birthday Mark Twain bookmark

Photocopy bookmark onto white, brown or blue copier paper.

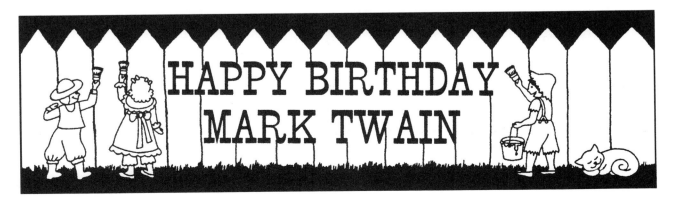

Foldout Table Display

Follow "Foldout Table Display" directions on p. 5–6, using white poster board. Cut top of display in a zigzag pattern. Draw lines on fence with a brown marker. Staple grass, children and cat to the display.

Display books, videos, audio tapes and/or CD-ROMs on works by Mark Twain.

Selected books by Mark Twain

The Celebrated Jumping Frog of Calaveras County and Other Sketches
The Innocents Abroad, or the New Pilgrims Progress
Mark Twain's Autobiography
The Innocents at Home
Roughing It
The Curious Dream; and Other Sketches
The Gilded Age: A Tale of Today
Mark Twain's Sketches, New and Old
The Adventures of Tom Sawyer
Old Times on the Mississippi
An Idle Excursion
The Tramp Abroad
The Prince and the Pauper
The Adventures of Huckleberry Finn
A Connecticut Yankee in King Arthur's Court
Pudd'nhead Wilson, A Tale
Following the Equator
The Man That Corrupted Hadleyburg and Other Stories
What Is Man?
Mark Twain's Speeches
The Mysterious Stranger: A Romance

Kids Can Make It!

Enlarge child with blank face onto an 8½" x 11" white paper and outline with black, round-tip felt marker. Photocopy child onto white construction paper. Have children draw themselves onto the blank child. Color and cut out children. Staple to bulletin board along side Tom, Becky and Huck.

Jerry Pinkney

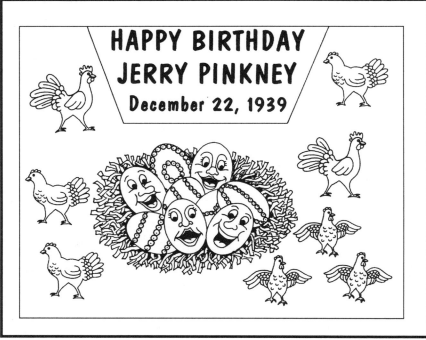

Bulletin board is based on *The Talking Eggs*

Directions ▼   Patterns on p. 55

1. BACKGROUND: Cover bulletin board by cutting white craft paper to the same size and stapling to board.

2. BORDER: Cut 3"-wide strips of green craft paper and staple to the perimeter of board.

3. BANNER: Enlarge banner onto green craft paper. Outline and fill in letters with black marker. Cut out banner and staple to bulletin board.

3. STRAW: Cut yellow construction paper into thin strips. Staple several layers of paper strips to bulletin board to make a nest.

4. EGGS and CHICKENS: Enlarge eggs and chickens onto white craft paper and outline with black marker. Color chickens with various bright colors such as green and purple. Glue sequins onto plain eggs. Cut out chickens and eggs, then staple to board.

Supplies ▼

Materials you need

- green craft paper for the banner and border
- yellow construction paper for the straw
- white craft paper for the background, eggs and chickens
- black, yellow, red, orange, bright blue, light green, light purple wide-tip, felt markers
- sequins
- white glue

Tools you need

- opaque or overhead projector
- photocopy machine
- scissors
- stapler
- pins

Jerry Pinkney

Jerry Pinkney was born in Philadelphia on December 22, 1939. As a youngster, he worked at a local newspaper stand and always took along his sketch pad and pencils to draw the store display windows and the people passing by.

One day, a cartoonist noticed him drawing and invited Jerry to his studio. He gave him supplies and talked to him about making a career as an illustrator. Through grade school, Jerry continued to draw as much as he could, taking drawing and painting classes after school. Upon graduating from high school, Pinkney earned a scholarship to the Philadelphia College of Art.

In 1960, Pinkney married and moved to Boston. He started his career illustrating studio cards. A few years later, he was employed by a design studio and illustrated his first book, an African folktale. In 1964, Pinkney and two other artists opened Kaleidoscope Studio. To date, Pinkney has illustrated dozens of books and works as a freelance artist.

Jerry Pinkney has received many awards for his work, including a 1979 Certificate of Achievement from the NAACP in Westchester. *The Talking Eggs* and *John Henry* were named Caldecott Honor Books; *Childtimes* won a *Boston Globe-Horn Book* Honor Book in 1980; *Patchwork Quilt* won the 1986 Coretta Scott King Award for illustration; as did *Half a Moon and One Whole Star* (1987) and *Minty: A Story of Young Harriet Tubman* (1997). *Quilt* also won a Christopher Award.

In all of Jerry Pinkney's work, the underlying theme has been the same: capturing the dignity of the human spirit, no matter how or when or where it is found.

Happy Birthday Jerry Pinkney bookmark

Photocopy bookmark onto white, yellow or green copier paper.

Foldout Table Display ⭥

Follow "Foldout Table Display" directions on p. 5–6, using white poster board. Staple straw and eggs to bulletin boards. Add baskets of plastic eggs and straw to display.

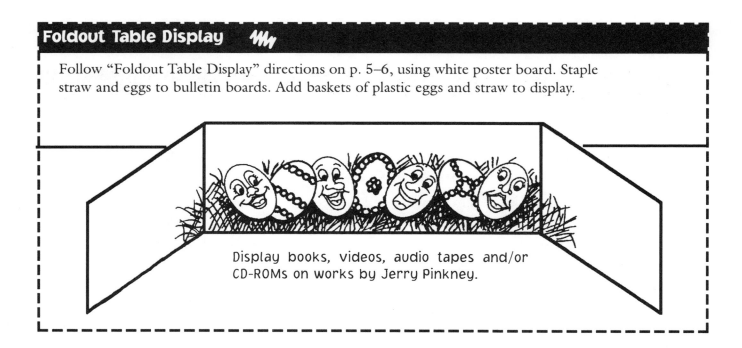

Display books, videos, audio tapes and/or CD-ROMs on works by Jerry Pinkney.

Selected books illustrated by Jerry Pinkney

Mirandy and Brother Wind. Pat McKissack.

Sam and the Tigers. Julius Lester.

Minty: A Story of Harriet Tubman. Allen Schroeder.

The Jungle Book. Rudyard Kipling.

John Henry. Julius Lester.

The Last Tales of Uncle Remus.

The Sunday Outing. Gloria Pinkney.

I Want to Be. Thylias Moss.

Drylongso. Virginia Hamilton.

In for Winter Out for Spring. Arnold Adoff.

Rabbit Makes a Monkey of a Lion. Verna Aardema.

Turtle in July. Marilyn Singer.

The Talking Eggs. Robert San Souci.

Half Moon and Whole Star. Crescent Dragonwagon.

The Patchwork Quilt. Valerie Flournoy.

Childtimes, Eloise Greenfield.

Roll of Thunder. Mildred Taylor.

Kids Can Make It!

Enlarge plain egg onto an 8½" x 11" white paper and outline with a black round-tip felt marker. Photocopy egg onto white construction paper. Have children draw their faces on eggs or decorate with sequins. Cut out eggs and staple to bulletin board or hang around the room.

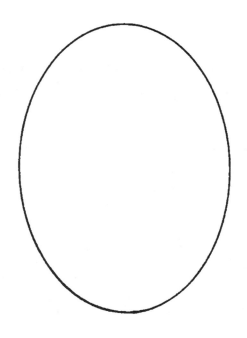

Jerry Pinkney
Talking Egg patterns

Dinosaur Days

Directions ▼   Patterns on p. 59

1. BACKGROUND: Cover board with yellow craft paper.

2. VOLCANO and FOREGROUND: Enlarge volcano and foreground onto bulletin board and outline with white chalk. Using a sponge, paint volcano and foreground with orange tempera paint. Crumple sheets of foil into the shape of lava and staple to board. Paint the lava with red tempera paint.

3. TITLE: Enlarge title onto white craft paper (p. 57). Outline letters with black marker. Cut out letters and staple to bulletin board.

4. TYRANNOSAURUS: Enlarge Tyrannosaurus onto green craft paper and outline with black marker. Color Tyrannosaurus with colored markers. Cut out and staple to bulletin board.

5. PTERANODONS: Enlarge pteranodons onto an 8½" x 11" sheet of paper and outline with a round-tip black felt marker. Photocopy pteranodons onto purple or green copier paper. Cut out pteranodons and staple to bulletin board.

Supplies ▼

Materials you need
- yellow craft paper for the background
- white craft paper for the title
- green craft paper for the Tyrannosaurus
- purple or green construction paper for Pteranodons
- black wide-tip, felt marker
- colored wide-tip, felt markers
- white chalk
- orange and red tempera paint
- aluminum foil

Tools you need
- opaque or overhead projector
- photocopy machine
- 1" flat-tip brush
- sponge
- scissors
- stapler
- pins

Dinosaur Days

Something About Dinosaurs

More than 200 million years ago, a new group of animals appeared on Earth—dinosaurs. The word itself means "terrible lizard." Like today's lizards, dinosaurs were cold-blooded reptiles with scaly skin who laid eggs. Some were fierce meat-eaters; while others ate only plants. No one has ever seen a dinosaur because, for some unknown reason, they all became extinct over 60 million years ago—before man walked the Earth. Yet, for those 150 million years, dinosaurs ruled the world.

Remains of dinosaurs were first discovered in England in the 1820s. By the 1840s, the great comparative anatomist Richard Owen gave them the name "Dinosauria." Owen recognized the uniqueness of their great size, their habits, their upright posture, and the fact that there were at least five vertebrae in their hip girdles. But it was not until the exploration of the western United States in the 1880s, where complete dinosaur skeletons were visible in the barren badlands, that dinosaurs were recognized as having been largely two-legged or bipedal—an unusual stance for a reptile and one that led to much speculation about their locomotion, behavior, and physiology.

The **Sauropods** (Jurassic Period: 185–64 million years ago) were the longest, tallest and heaviest of all dinosaurs and the largest land animals ever known. Based on fossil remains first discovered in 1877 in Colorado and later in Utah, Sauropods were four-legged, plant eaters that grew over 100 feet long and weight more than 225 tons. **Carnosaurs** (Jurassic Period: 150-140 million years ago) were the "giant killers." These two-legged, meat-eating hunters grew to as much as 36 feet long and may have weighted up to two tons and are probably the fiercest hunters in history.

There are two popular theories that explain the disappearance of the dinosaurs: 1. A large meteor (about 5–10 miles wide) collided with the earth. The impact created an explosion of dust particles that blocked out the sun for several years. This would have caused vegetation (the source of food for the plant eaters) to die; and then the death of the plant eaters (the source of food for the meat eaters); 2. By 64 million years ago, the continents had separated extensively, thus separating the dinosaurs who had been free to roam literally over most of the earth. There was felt to be a gradual change in the weather toward a cooler, less tropical climate, which changed the amount of available food. Thus, the limitation of habitat, the change in weather and the subsequent reduction in available food, may have brought an end to the dinosaur.

The fossils left behind tell a story that has fascinated children, adults and scientists ever since—and has served as an inspiration for books, movies and television worldwide.

Title/ Bookmark

Photocopy and enlarge **title**. See p. 56 for bulletin board directions.
Photocopy **bookmark** onto and have children color.

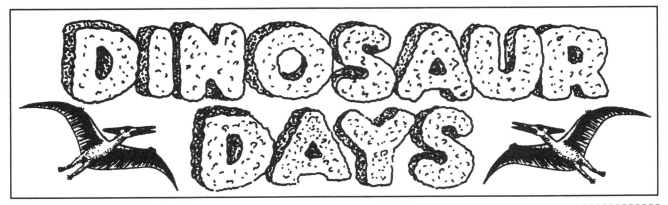

Foldout Table Display

Follow "Foldout Table Display" directions on p. 5–6, using yellow poster board. Cut a rough edge along top portion of display. Paint display following directions in step 2 on p. 56. Staple Tyrannosaurus to display.

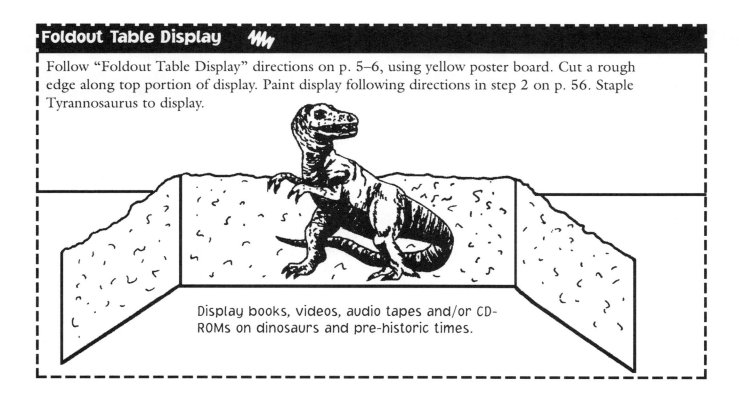

Display books, videos, audio tapes and/or CD-ROMs on dinosaurs and pre-historic times.

Some Books About Dinosaurs

The New Book of Dinosaurs. David Unwin, 1997.

Allosaurus and Other Jurassic Meat-eaters. Daniel Cohen, 1996.

Dinosaur Worlds: New Dinosaurs and New Discoveries. Don Lessem, 1996.

How Dinosaurs Came to Be. Patricia Lauber, 1996.

Dino-Trekking: the Ultimate Dinosaur Lover's Trek. Kelly Miner Halls, 1996.

The Search for Dinosaurs. Dougal Dixon, 1995.

Dinosaurs. Scott Steedman, 1995.

165 Million Years of Dinosaurs. Francois Gohier, 1995.

The Visual Dictionary of Prehistoric Life. 1995.

The Magic School Bus in the Time of the Dinosaur. Joanne Cole, 1994.

Incredible Dinosaurs. Christopher Maynard, 1994.

What Color Is That Dinosaur? Lowell Dingus, 1994.

My Visit to the Dinosaurs. Aliki, 1994.

Kids Can Make It!

Photocopy pteranodon on p. 59 onto white construction paper and have children color and cut out a pteranodon. Fold pteranodon in half and punch a hole in the center just above the fold. When you open up the pteranodon, you will have two parallel holes. Slip an 8" length of yarn or elastic through holes and tie to child's wrist. Have children raise and lower pteranodon to make wings flap.

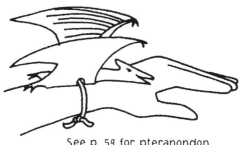

See p. 59 for pteranondon pattern

Use for pteranondon
craft on p. 58

Ancient Mythology

Patterns on p. 63

Directions ▼

1. BACKGROUND: Cover bulletin board by cutting bright blue craft paper to the same size and stapling to board.

2. BANNER: Enlarge banner design and stars onto yellow craft paper. Outline letters and design with black marker. Fill in letters and border with black marker. Cut out banner and stars, then staple banner to bulletin board.

3. ANCIENT MYTHOLOGY FIGURES: Enlarge ancient mythological figures onto white craft paper and outline with black marker. Using black, light green, yellow, orange, red, light brown and bright blue markers, color in designs. Cut out figures and staple to bulletin board. Featured in the bulletin board above are the Greek goddess of crafts, war and wisdom Athena; the Egyptian God Anubis, escort to the afterworld; the Aztec God of the wind and arts, Quetzalcoatl; and the mythical Greek flying horse, Pegasus.

Supplies ▼

Materials you need

- bright blue craft paper for the background
- bright yellow craft paper for the banner
- white craft paper for mythology figures
- black, light green, yellow, orange, red, light brown and bright blue, wide-tip, felt markers

Tools you need

- opaque or overhead projector
- photocopy machine
- scissors
- stapler
- pins

Ancient Mythology

Societies throughout time have developed stories to explain the world around them. These stories often have become part of the society's religious life, and it is the religious rituals associated with the stories that have characterized them as "myth" and separated them from "folktales" or "legends."

Myths tend to divide into two groups: **creation myths** and **explanatory myths**. Creation myths try to explain the creation of man, the origin of the world, the birth of super powers or the origin of gods and goddesses. Explanatory myths, on the other hand, try to explain natural phenomena. In many ways, these tales represent early versions of scientific theory.

Myths generally portray in symbolic language the basic assumptions of a culture. For example, the earliest information we have about Egypt comes from **Egyptian mythology.** Hieroglyphics on the walls of tombs, dating back to 3000 BC, tells us much about the culture's daily life and religious rituals. In the hieroglyphics, the two are difficult to separate. The Egyptians believed in a family of nine gods, each playing a different role in creating and explaining life in ancient Egypt.

Greek mythology, which appeared in Hesiod's *Theogony* and Homer's *Iliad and Odyssey*, dates from about 700 BC. The Greek myths are rich in drama and their stories are still meaningful to modern times. **Roman mythology,** which came into its own by about 500 BC, was based largely on the mythic structure developed by the Greeks. One of the main differences between the two cultures, however, is that the Romans used myths as a way to explain the origin and history of their nation.

A wide variety of mythologies developed among the diverse peoples of **Africa.** The majority of these concerned prominent features in nature, such as mountains, rivers and the sun. Most of the cultures believed that virtually everything in nature contains a spirit, which could be either friendly or unfriendly.

The **Aztec Indians** of central Mexico developed one of the most interesting Indian mythologies. As the Aztecs conquered neighboring tribes, they incorporated the myths and divinities of the other tribes into their own explanations of the world and its origin. Human sacrifice was also common practice among the Aztecs. Most of the victims were prisoners of war; nonetheless, the Aztecs believed the sacrifice would serve them well in the eyes of their deities. The chief Aztec god was Huitzilopochtli, the God of War. Other important deities represented the arts and agriculture.

Myths, in their many forms, have worked their way into modern thought as a standard part of academic disciplines: anthropology, history, comparative literature, philosophy, psychology, history of religions, political science, and structural linguistics. Scholars also point to today's cultural obsessions and draw parallels to their mythic origins.

Banner/ Bookmark

Photocopy and enlarge for banner. Photocopy bookmark onto blue, orange or yellow paper.

Foldout Table Display

Follow "Foldout Table Display" directions on p. 5–6, using bright blue poster board. Enlarge Pegasus onto white poster board and stars onto yellow construction paper. Outline Pegasus and stars with black marker. Cut out Pegasus and stars, then staple to display. Use photos or replicas of artifacts, such as figures, crafts and/or musical instruments from ancient civilizations.

Display books, videos, audio tapes and/or CD-ROMs on ancient civilizations. There are also many stories of modern-day "adventure heroes" that are based on these early myths, including Hercules and Xena.

Some Books About Myths

Goddesses, Heroes and Shamans. 1997.

Mythical Birds and Beasts from Many Lands. Margaret Mayo, 1997.

Near Myths: Dug Up and Dusted Off. Robert Kraus, 1996.

Dragons: Truth, Myth and Legend. David Passes, 1993.

In the Beginning: Creation Stories from Around the World. Virginia Hamilton, 1988.

Gods, Stars, and Computers. Malcom Weiss, 1980.

D'Aulaires' Norse Gods and Giants. Ingri an Edgar Parin D'Aulaire, 1967.

D'Aulaires' Book of Greek Myths. Ingrid and Edgar Parin D'Aulaire, 1962.

Kids Can Make It!

Photocopy figures onto white construction paper. Have children color and cut out figures. Glue figures to craft sticks to make "Mythological Puppets." Figures and stars can also be uses to make mobiles.

Medieval Kingdoms

Directions ▼   Patterns on p. 67

1. BACKGROUND: Cover bulletin board by cutting bright blue craft paper to the same size and stapling to board. Cut a 12"-wide section of green craft paper the same length as the board for the grass. Staple green craft paper to the bulletin board.

2. BANNER: Enlarge title banner onto yellow craft paper. Enlarge small banners each onto red, blue and yellow construction paper. Outline letters and design with black marker. Color in letters and border with black marker. Cut out banners and glue small banners to title banner. Staple banners to bulletin board.

3. KNIGHTS: Enlarge knights and jousting poles onto white craft paper and outline with black marker. Using markers color in designs. Cut out knights and poles. Glue poles onto knights. Staple to bulletin board.

Supplies ▼

Materials you need

- bright blue craft paper for the background
- bright yellow craft paper for the banner
- green craft paper for the grass
- white craft paper for the knights
- yellow, blue and red construction paper for the small banners
- black, green, yellow, red and bright blue, wide-tip, felt markers
- white glue

Tools you need

- opaque or overhead projector
- photocopy machine
- scissors
- stapler
- pins

Medieval Kingdoms

Something About the Middle Ages

Medieval Kingdoms grew up during the Middle Ages—a period extending from the end of the Roman Empire to the early 1500s. By the middle of AD 400, the great Roman Empire was weakening and rapidly losing control over Europe and the Middle East. Invaders from England and Northern Europe—later known as the legendary knights, replete in armor, shields and swords—had little trouble conquering the unprotected towns and villages.

Tales of heroism and chivalry abound as invaders formed their own kingdoms. These large estates or "manors" were held by landlords or "lords," and were supported by the labor "serfs." Each kingdom was secured by their lord's army. These wars kept the kingdoms isolated from one another, bringing trade and communication to a virtual halt. Education and cultural activities practically ceased. Living conditions were deplorable, particularly for the peasants, who were denied basic human rights by their lords and suffered in poverty and disease. The agonizing Black Death, a sweeping epidemic of the bubonic plague (1347-1350), killed one-fourth of the European population and epitomized the dreadful conditions of the period. The Christian Church became the most powerful focus of these peoples' lives. But by the early 1500s, even the Church became the object of rebellion, giving rise to the Protestant Reformation and the Age of the Renaissance.

Until the middle of the 1400s, scholars considered the medieval period that of cultural stagnation—once referred to as the Dark Ages—a time caught between the glory of classical antiquity and its rebirth in the Renaissance. However after 1450, known as the High Middle Ages, there was a period that was very active intellectually and artistically. New educational institutions, such as cathedral and monastic schools, prospered, and the first universities were established. Advanced degrees in medicine, law, and theology were offered, and in each field inquiry was intense. Both religious and civil law were systematized. Innovations took place in the creative arts as well. As the common people became literate, a new "romantic" literature arose, both in Latin and in the native languages. In painting, great attention was given to the emotional extremes. In architecture, the intricate, delicate and ornate Romanesque style was perfected.

One of the heroic figures to emerge from this time was the knight—a mounted man-at-arms of medieval Europe, who served a king or other feudal superior, usually in return for the tenure of a tract of land. The knight usually swore to be brave, loyal, and courteous and to protect the defenseless. After the fifteenth century, knighthood would be conferred on civilians as a reward for public services.

Banner/Bookmark

Enlarge and photocopy **banner**. Directions for colors on p. 64.
Photocopy **bookmark** onto blue, red or yellow copier paper.

Foldout Table Display

Follow "Foldout Table Display" directions on p. 5–6, using green poster board. Staple knights to display. Use photos or replicas of knights, kings, queens, castles, musical instruments, art work and other items from medieval times.

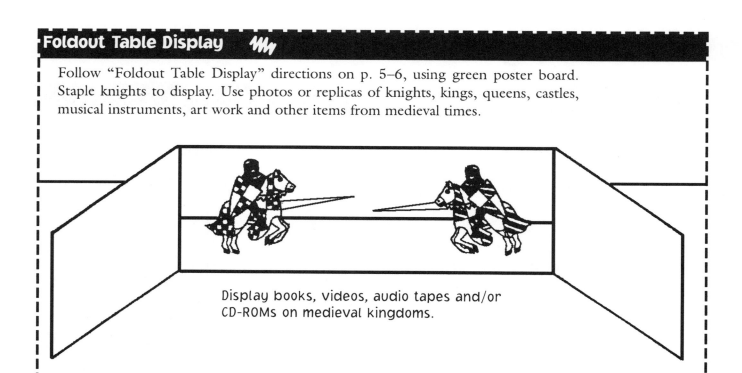

Display books, videos, audio tapes and/or CD-ROMs on medieval kingdoms.

Some Books About the Middle Ages

History of the Ancient and Medieval World. 1996.

The Middle Ages. Fiona MacDonald, 1993.

The Knight at Dawn. Mary Pope Osborne, 1993.

Richard the Lion Hearted. Catherine Storr, 1989.

Looking at a Castle. Brian Davison, 1987.

Charlemagne. Susan Banfield, 1986.

Knights. Julek Heller, 1982.

Living in Castle Times. Robyn Gee, 1982.

Gudrun. Alma Koenig, 1979.

Catherine the Great. Miriam Kochan, 1977.

The Time Traveler Book of Knights and Castles. Judy Hindley, 1976.

Life in a Medieval Castle. Joseph Gies, 1974.

Kids Can Make It!

Photocopy knights and jousting poles on p. 67 onto white construction paper. Have children color and cut out figures. Glue figures to craft sticks to make Knight Puppets.

Following the Great Explorers

Directions ▼   Patterns on p. 71

1. BACKGROUND: Cover bulletin board by cutting white craft paper to the same size and stapling to board. Dilute coffee with water. Using paper towels dab coffee onto white paper to make it look old.

2. BANNER, TITLE and BORDER: Enlarge banner, title and border onto bulletin board and outline with black marker. Fill in letters and border with black marker.

3. MAP: Enlarge map onto board and outline with black marker. Dilute green tempera paint with water and sponge onto land masses on map.

4. EXPLORERS: Enlarge explorers onto white craft paper and outline with black marker. Color explorers using markers. Cut out and staple to board. Draw each dashed line using a different color of marker and pattern. Featured in the bulletin board above are Leif Ericson, Marco Polo, Sir Francis Drake and Christopher Columbus. You may also want to label the explorers.

Supplies ▼

Materials you need

- white or tan craft paper for the background
- white craft paper for the Explorers
- black, blue, green, red and yellow wide-tip, felt markers
- coffee
- paper towels
- green tempera paint

Tools you need

- opaque or overhead projector
- photocopy machine
- scissors
- stapler
- pins
- 1" flat-tip brush
- sponge

Following the Great Explorers

No matter what period, what purpose, what means or what destination, the challenge of the unknown has called explorers to its vast frontiers. In 2,500 BC, it was the Babylonian and Egyptian traders who traveled as far south as the Indian Ocean and as far west as the Mediterranean Sea. The ancient Greeks learned more about geography by the AD 400s than any other civilization, mainly through exploration of the Mediterranean, Europe and Africa.

In the Middle Ages, it was the Vikings who crafted some of the finest sailing vessels to seek more land and food for their people, settling in areas now known as England, Scotland, Ireland and Iceland. About AD1000, the most famous Viking, Lief Ericson, led an expedition to what is now Newfoundland.

Yet, it wasn't until the 1400s that world exploration reached an unprecedented peak. Kings and queens spent fortunes seeking more land, more riches and more power. The accomplishments of the Great Age of European Exploration are still unmatched by any time period since.

Today, this same spirit of discovery lives on as great explorers continue to probe the limits of human understanding, in a wide range of frontiers: science, medicine, space, physics, oceanography and communications. Discovery and exploration are an essential part of the human spirit.

Great Explorers Bookmark

Photocopy bookmark onto tan, blue or green copier paper.

Foldout Table Display

Follow "Foldout Table Display" directions on p. 5–6, using white poster board. Give poster board an aged look by following the directions in no. 1 on p. 68. Staple explorers to display. Draw dashed lines onto display using colored markers.

Display books, videos, audio tapes and/or CD-ROMs on explorers and their times.

Some Books About Exploration

Follow the Dream. Peter Sis, 1996.

The Search for the East. Peter Chrisp, 1993.

Explorers and Exploration: The Best Resources. Ann Welton, 1993.

The Spanish Conquests in the New World. Peter Chrisp, 1993.

Vasco da Gama and the Portuguese Explorers. Rabecca Stefoff, 1993.

Roald Amundsen and the Quest for the South Pole. Leo Flaherty, 1992.

Accidental Explorers: Surprises and Side Trips. Rebecca Stefoff, 1992.

The Discoverers of America. Harold Faber, 1992.

Women of the World: Women Travelers and Explorers. Rebecca Srefoff, 1992.

The Nina, the Piñta, and the Santa Maria. Dennis Fradin, 1991.

Meriwether Lewis and William Clark. David Petersen, 1988.

Where Do You Think You're Going Christopher Columbus. Jean Friz, 1976.

Kids Can Make It!

Photocopy explorers on p. 71 onto white construction paper and have children color and cut out. Glue craft sticks to the backs of explorers to make puppets.

Pirates on the High Seas

Directions ▼   Patterns on p. 75

1. BACKGROUND: Cover entire board with light blue craft paper.

2. BANNER: Enlarge banner (p. 73) onto white craft paper. Outline and fill in border and flag with black marker. Outline and fill in letters with red marker. Cut out banner and staple to bulletin board.

3. WAVES: Enlarge waves onto dark blue craft paper. Outline design in white pencil. Mix a few drops of green tempera paint into white tempera paint. Sponge paint onto top of waves. Let dry then cut out waves. Staple waves to board leaving unstapled at the top of the bottom row of waves.

4. SHIPS: Enlarge ships onto brown craft paper and outline with black marker. Cut out ships and fold along dashed lines. Glue back and front of ships to sides of ships. Cut ½" strips from brown craft paper for the masts. Cut large squares from white craft paper for the sails. Staple ships and masts to bulletin board. Fold top and bottom sails over 1". Curve sails by bringing top and bottom closer together, then staple to masts. Cut flags from black construction

Supplies ▼

Materials you need
- light blue craft paper for the background
- dark blue craft paper for the waves
- white craft paper for the banner and the sails
- brown craft paper for the ships and masts
- black construction paper for the flags
- black and red wide-tip, felt markers
- white and green tempera paint
- white glue
- white pencil

Tools you need
- opaque or overhead projector
- photocopy machine
- scissors
- pins
- sponge
- stapler

paper and draw skull and crossbones with white pencil. Glue flags to masts.

Pirates on the High Seas

Something About the Pirates

The romantic and adventurous episodes attributed to pirates on the high seas have been vastly overrated. Upon closer look, the image of a dashing, swashbuckling buccaneer gives way to common criminals out to get rich by attacking ships and robbing their captain and crew. Most pirates endured miserable lives and died of wounds or disease. They often fought with their own crew members and occasionally were marooned or forced to abandon ship.

Piracy has been a problem on the open seas since ancient times. However, the greatest period of piracy took place from 1500–1700, during the times of greatest sea travel and exploration on the Mediterranean and Caribbean Seas. The most famous pirates of this age were: Arouj and his brother Khair-ed-Din Barbarossa, Henry Morgan, Blackbeard, and William Kidd. Most pirates were men, but there were a few female pirates as well.

Pirates were also known by other names, including: corsairs, filibusters, freebooters, ladrones, pickaroons, sea rovers and buccaneers. In the seventeenth century, the name "buccaneer" described a very specific group of English, Dutch, and French seafaring thieves who had settled on the Caribbean island of Hispaniola. The buccaneers robbed ships carrying gold and silver on their way back to Spain from North and South America. They also raided the seaport towns in Hispaniola, taking cattle from Spanish plantations. They dried the meat on grills known in French as "boucan" (hence their name); and sold the dried meat to other vessels. The most famous buccaneer, Sir Henry Morgan, was from England. Several buccaneers wrote tales of their adventures, which inspired further exploration in the New World.

There was some honor among these thieves. Despite their uncivilized ways, pirates developed regulations to govern their ships and a code of punishment for breaking these rules. They also set pay scales to carve out each person's share of the "booty," or stolen goods.

It wasn't until after the 1850s, when countries could support naval ships more powerful than those of the pirates, that these sea rovers no longer posed a threat to ocean passage.

Banner/Bookmark ≪≪≪

Enlarge and photocopy **banner**. See directions on p.72 for colors.
Photocopy **bookmark** onto blue, white or red copier paper.

Foldout Table Display

Follow "Foldout Table Display" directions on p. 5–6, using light blue poster board. Staple ships and waves to display. Add models of ships, treasure chests, pirate hats and fish nets to display.

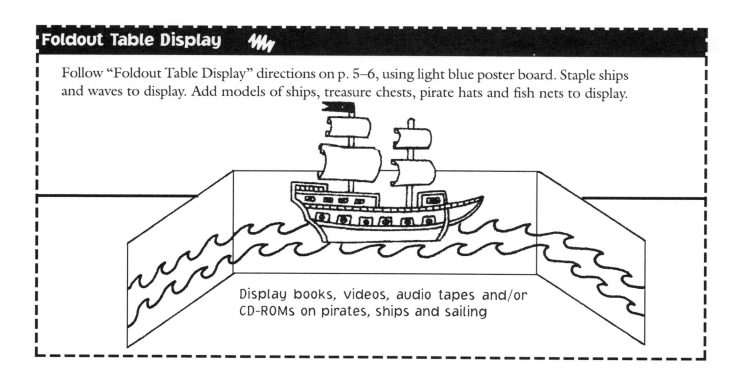

Display books, videos, audio tapes and/or CD-ROMs on pirates, ships and sailing

Some Books About Pirates

Pirates. Scott Steedman, 1996.

Pirates and Treasures. Savior Pirotta, 1995.

Pirates. Stewart Ross, 1995.

The Pirates Handbook. Margarette Lincoln, 1995.

Pirate. Richard Platt, 1994.

Captain Grey. Avi, 1993.

Pirates: Robbers of the High Seas. Gail Gibbons, 1993.

Pirates. Albert Marrin, 1989.

The Sea Rovers: Pirates, Privateers, and Buccaneers. John Gilbert, 1984.

The Last Battle. Leonard Wibberley, 1976.

Old Hasdrubal and the Pirates. Berthe Amoss, 1971.

Pirate's Island. John Rowe Townsend, 1968.

Treasure Island. Robert Louis Stevenson, 1939.

Kids Can Make It!

Photocopy ship on p.75 onto brown construction paper. Have children make ships following in step 4 directions on p. 72. Glue ships to sheets of blue construction paper. Display ships onto bulletin board to make an exciting pirate scene.

See p. 72 for directions and p. 75 for pattern.

Pirate ship pattern

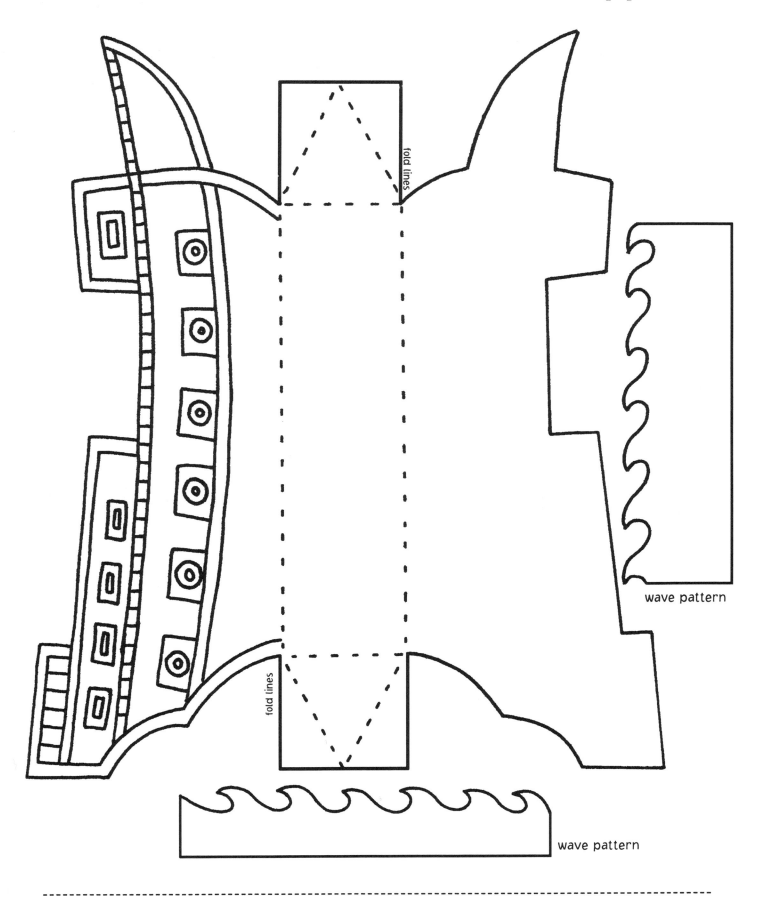

fold lines

fold lines

wave pattern

wave pattern

Pilgrims & Indians

Directions ▼   Patterns on p. 79

1. BACKGROUND: Cover bulletin board by cutting orange craft paper to the same size and stapling to board.

2. BANNER: Enlarge banner (p. 77) onto white craft paper. Outline letters and designs with black marker. Color in letters with black marker and corn with green and yellow markers. Cut out banner and staple to bulletin board.

3. CORN: Enlarge corn onto green poster board and outline design in black marker. Glue popcorn kernels onto green corn and staple to bulletin board.

4. FIGURES: Enlarge figures onto white craft paper and outline with black marker. Using markers, color figures red, yellow, green, blue, white, skin tone and black. Cut out figures and staple to board.

Supplies ▼

Materials you need

- orange craft paper for the background
- white craft paper for the figures and banner
- green poster board for the corn
- pencil
- black, red, yellow, green, blue and skin tone wide-tip, felt markers
- white glue
- popcorn kernels

Tools you need

- opaque or overhead projector
- photocopy machine
- scissors
- stapler
- pins

Pilgrims & Indians

Something About the Early Settlers

The Pilgrims were early English settlers of North America. The first group of Pilgrims landed at what is now Plymouth, Massachusetts, in 1620, establishing the second permanent settlement in the New World, the first being Jamestown (1607). Plymouth Colony was established on the rocky western shore of Cape Cod Bay and remained intact until 1691, when it became part of the Massachusetts Bay Colony.

The story of this colony and its people has become a lesson in how courage, perseverance and hard work can create a home in a hostile world. In the early 1600s, there was a rebellion in the Church of England. One segment of the Church, the Puritans, sought reforms that would "purify" their religion. Another group, the Separatists, broke away from the Church altogether. Separatism was illegal in England, and in 1606, a small band of Separatists fled to Amsterdam, Holland.

As foreigners, Separatists could not buy land or work in skilled trades. They heard stories of "America" and decided to set up an English colony in the New Land. In September, 1620, 41 members of the congregation along with 61 other English people, set sail on the *Mayflower*. (Their other ship, the *Speedwell*, proved unseaworthy and the voyagers crowded into one boat.) It was a miserable passage, but on November 20, the *Mayflower* landed at what is now Plymouth, Massachusetts, establishing Plymouth Colony along Cape Cod Bay.

The first year was difficult. They lost almost half the colony to starvation, exposure and disease. Yet, the Pilgrims cooperated and learned from a local tribe of Native Americans, the Samoset, how to survive by catching fish and using the remains as fertilizer in planting corn, pumpkins and beans. They also formulated a code of conduct, known as the "Mayflower Compact," which organized a representational democracy and became a model for future colonial settlements.

Autumn of 1621 brought a bountiful harvest, and Governor William Bradford declared a three-day festival, The New England Thanksgiving, featuring cornbread, duck, eel, goose, leeks, shellfish, venison, watercress and wine. The Thanksgiving holiday has been a cherished American tradition ever since, as it commemorates how working together in peace can bring a harvest of plenty to our lives.

Banner/ Bookmark ◄◄◄◄

Enlarge and photocopy banner. See p. 76 for directions on how to color.
Photocopy bookmark onto orange, yellow or light brown copier paper. Have children color.

Foldout Table Display

Follow "Foldout Table Display" directions on p. 5–6, using light blue poster board. Cut grass from green craft paper and staple to display. Staple figures to display.

Display books, video tapes, audio tapes and/or CD/ROMs on Pilgrims, Native Americans and Thanksgiving. Add pumpkins, Indian corn and figures or pictures of Pilgrims and Indians.

Books About Indians & Pilgrims

The Story of Squanto, First Friend to the Pilgrims. Cathy Dubowski, 1997.

The Pilgrims at Plymouth. Lucille Penner, 1996.

Tapenum's Day: a Wampanoag Indian Boy in Pilgrims. Kate Waters, 1996. *The Encyclopedia of Native America.* Trudy Griffin-Pierce, 1995.

The Iroquois. Virginia Sneve, 1995.

The Shawnees: People of the Eastern Woodlands. Laurie O'Neill, 1995.

The Black Feet. Theresa Lacy, 1995.

The Seminoles. Virginia Sneve, 1994.

The Mohawk Indians. Jane Hubbard-Brown, 1993.

The First Thanksgiving. Jean Craighead George and illustrated by Thomas Locker, 1993.

N.C. Wyeth's Pilgrims. Robert San Souci and illustrated by N.C. Wyeth 1991.

The Powhatan tribes. Christian Feest, 1990.

Hiawatha. Henry Wadsworth Longfellow, illustrated by Susan Jeffers, 1983.

Kids Can Make It!

Kids Can Make It!

Photocopy figures on p. 79 onto white construction paper. Have children color and cut out figures. Glue figures to craft sticks to make Pilgrim and Indian puppets. Display puppets on bulletin board, glue onto place cards or make a puppet show.

Pilgrims and Indians patterns

corn pattern

Westward Ho!

Patterns on p. 82-83

Directions ▼

1. BACKGROUND: Cover bulletin board with light blue craft paper. Cut a 12"- and a 30"-wide section of green craft paper the same length as bulletin board for the grass. Cut the top of each strip of green craft paper to look like blades of grass. Staple green 30"-wide craft paper to the bottom of the bulletin board. Staple green 12"-wide craft paper on top of 30"-wide craft paper at the bottom of bulletin board.

2. TITLE: Enlarge title onto bulletin board and outline letters with a pencil. Pin rope on top of letters with straight pins. Cut rope as needed.

3. WAGONS and CATTLE: Enlarge wagon and cattle onto brown craft paper and outline with black marker. Cut out wagons and cattle. Fold wagons and cattle along dashed lines. Glue front and back of wagon to sides of wagon. Glue wheels onto wagon. Cut a rectangle out of white construction paper and glue to sides of wagon to form top. Staple wagons and cattle to bulletin board. Glue yarn from wagon to cattle and then from cattle to cattle.

Supplies ▼

Materials you need

- light blue craft paper for the background
- green craft paper for the grass
- brown craft paper for the wagons and cattle
- white construction paper for the tops of wagons
- ¼" rope
- red yarn
- black wide-tip, felt marker
- white glue

Tools you need

- opaque or overhead projector
- photocopy machine
- scissors
- stapler
- pins

4. Border: Pin rope around perimeter of bulletin board.

Westward Ho!

Something About the Wild West

It is sometimes said that the American spirit was born in the Wild West. Hopefully, this refers to the inventiveness, courage and perseverance of the pioneers who sought adventure and opportunities in the uncharted territory; and is not a reference to the outlaws or cattle rustlers whose stories were romanticized in the legend and lore of an untamed wilderness.

The way West was not marked by a steady flow but a series of ebbs and flows of adventurers. Essentially, there were four periods in the nation's Manifest Destiny or settlement from sea to shining sea. In the 1760s, colonists pushed into the Appalachian highlands, despite French laws and battles waged by the American Indians. By 1783, communities had grown up as far west as the Mississippi, and settlers looked to the Federal government to establish forts and outposts for protection. During the early 1800s, traders, trappers and explorers ventured even farther west, staking claims in territories that American Indians felt strongly did not "belong" to anyone—particularly the settlers. By the 1850s, Americans had reached the Pacific. It was during the next 40 years that the West got its wild reputation.

For example, at Sutter's Mill in 1848, a sparkling rock set off an unprecedented fever for fortune: The California Gold Rush of 1849. Those that followed included adventurers from every walk of life. At the same time that cowboys and cattle barons were staking their claims in the open territory, farmers were planting roots and raising families directly in their path. Before long, the railroad and telegraph were speeding across the plains. And outlaws took whatever they could, without regard to lives or property. Watching it all were the First Americans, who made valiant but largely unsuccessful attempts to keep their Mother Land as it was. Perhaps "wild" is a bit mild in describing this period of American history. Clearly, this individualism is what characterizes the American spirit—and the conflict that comes with it.

Westward Ho! Bookmark

Photocopy bookmark onto a light-colored copier paper. Have children color bookmark.

Foldout Table Display

Follow "Foldout Table Display" directions on p. 5–6, using light blue poster board. Staple wagons, cattle and grass to the display.

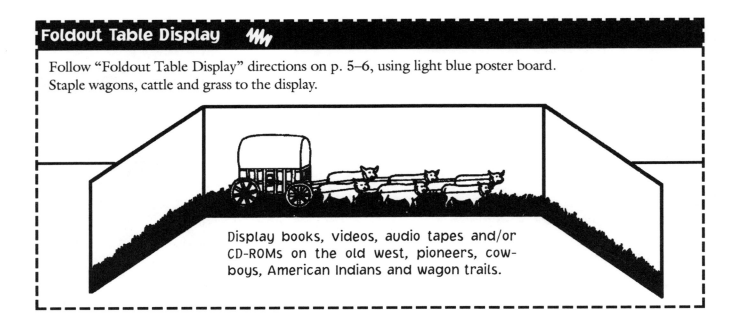

Display books, videos, audio tapes and/or CD-ROMs on the old west, pioneers, cowboys, American Indians and wagon trails.

Some Books About the West

Daniel Boone: Wilderness Pioneer. William Stanford, 1997.

Snowshoe Thompson. Nancy Levinson, 1996.

Buffalo Gals: Women of the Old West. Brandon Miller, 1995.

The Story of the Stagecoach Mary Fields. Robert Miller, 1995.

James Blackwourth. Sean Dolan, 1992.

Westward Ho, Ho, Ho. Peter Roop. 1996.

Facing West: A Story of the Oregon Trail. Kathleen Kudlinski, 1994.

Bound for Oregon. Jean Van Leeuwen, 1994.

The Oregon Trail. Conrad R. Stein, 1994.

A Frontier Fort on the Oregon Trail. Scott Steedman, 1993.

Western Wagon Trains. Tim McNeese, 1993.

The Oregon Trail. Leonard Eve Fisher, 1990.

Pioneer Cat. William Hooks, 1988.

If You Traveled West in a Covered Wagon. Ellen Leine, 1986.

Little House in the Big Woods. Laura Ingalls Wilder, 1953.

Sarah, Plain and Tall. Patricia MacLachlan, 1985.

Kids Can Make It!

Kids Can Make It!

Enlarge steer onto an 8½" x 11" sheet of white paper and outline with black, round-tip felt marker. Photocopy wagon and cattle onto brown construction paper. Have children make wagons by following directions on p. 80. Create a bulletin board wagon train.

See p. 80 for directions and p. 83 for wagon patterns.

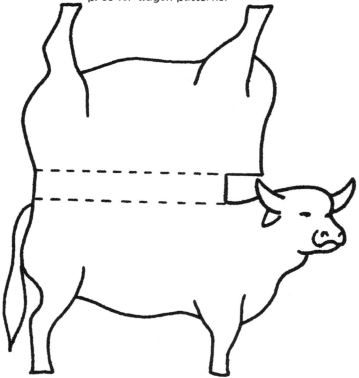

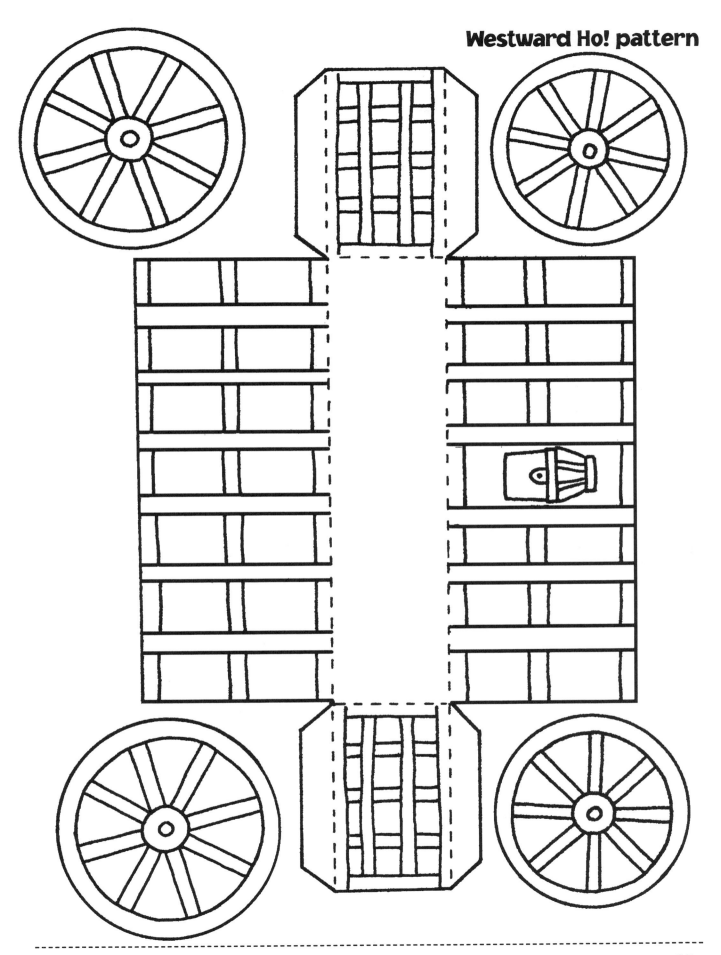

Space
The Final Frontier

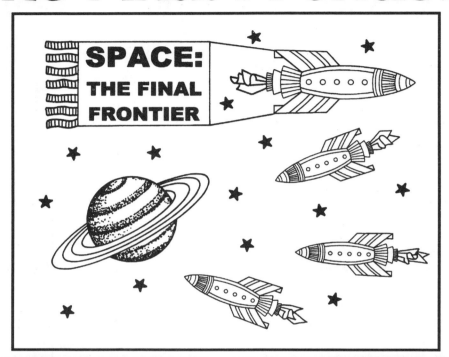

Directions ▼
Patterns on p. 87

1. BACKGROUND: Cover bulletin board by cutting black craft paper to the same size and stapling to board. Decorate background with gummed stars.

2. BANNER: Enlarge banner (p. 85) onto yellow craft paper. Outline and fill in letters with black marker. Cut out banner and 1" x8" strips of orange construction paper. Glue strips to left side of banner, then staple banner to bulletin board.

3. ROCKETS and SATURN: Enlarge rockets and Saturn onto white craft paper and outline with black marker. Using light green, yellow, orange, red, and bright blue markers, color rockets and Saturn, then cut out. Glue gold glitter onto rings of Saturn. Fold rockets in half lengthwise and along dashed lines. (p. 87) Scrunch up a piece of orange construction paper and staple to bottom of rocket. Staple rockets and Saturn to bulletin board. Attach yarn from banner to rocket.

Supplies ▼

Materials you need
- black craft paper for the background
- bright yellow craft paper for the banner
- white craft paper for the rockets and Saturn
- orange construction paper or tissue paper
- black, light green, yellow, orange, red, and bright blue, wide-tip, felt markers
- white glue
- gummed stars
- gold glitter
- orange or yellow yarn

Tools you need
- opaque or overhead projector
- photocopy machine
- scissors
- stapler
- pins

Space: The Final Frontier

Something About Space Books

Some consider space our most dramatic and compelling adventure—a dream since ancient times. Contemplation of space and space travel have fascinated scientists as well as writers of science fiction.

Space exploration, or astronautics, touches a wide range of fields of knowledge: physics, astronomy, mathematics, chemistry, biology, medicine, electronics, and meteorology. Space probes have provided a great new source of scientific data on the nature and origin of the solar system and the basis for new technologies that can be applied to our lives on earth. Earth-orbiting satellites, for instance, have improved global telecommunications, weather forecasting, navigation, military defense and the location of mineral resources.

The space age and practical astronautics commenced with the launching of *Sputnik 1* by the Soviet Union in October 1957 and of *Explorer 1* by the United States in January 1958. During the next three decades, more than 1800 spacecraft of all varieties have been launched into space.

This fascination with space exploration began with the Greek myths of Daedalus and the technology of flying, as well as the *True History* (about AD 160) written by Lucian of Samosata, complete with a trip to the moon. Imaginary voyages and tales of strange people in distant lands found new expression in the fourteenth-century book of travels written in French by Sir John Mandeville. Trips to the moon were also described by figures as diverse as the French writer Cyrano de Bergerac; the German astronomer Johannes Kepler in the seventeenth century; and the British philosopher and novelist William Godwin in the nineteenth century.

Space literature evolved further with French author Jules Verne, who dealt with geology and cave exploration in *Journey to the Center of the Earth* (1864), space travel in *From the Earth to the Moon* (1865) and *Off on a Comet* (1877). Authors of space literature during the first half of the twentieth century include Matthew Phipps Shiel (1865–1947) who wrote *The Purple Cloud* (1901); Olaf Stapledon (1886–1950) who wrote *Last and First Men* (1930), and C. S. Lewis (1898–1963), *Out of the Silent Planet* (1938). One of the most profound contributors to the subject is Ray Bradbury, whose works include *Martian Chronicles* (1950) as well as the inspiration for many film and television productions.

Banner/ Bookmark

Enlarge and copy **banner**. See p. 84 for directions on colors.
Photocopy **bookmark** onto blue, white or yellow copier paper, and allow students to color.

Foldout Table Display

Follow "Foldout Table Display" directions on p. 5–6, using bright blue poster board. Enlarge rocket onto white poster board and follow the directions in step 3 on p. 84. Sponge white tempera paint onto display to make clouds and decorate sky with gummed stars. Staple rocket to display. Cover display table with aluminum foil. Use photos or replicas of space craft, astronauts, and solar system to enhance display.

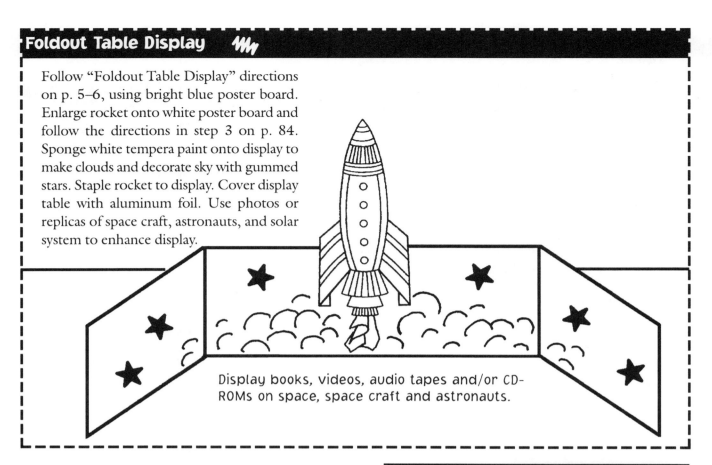

Display books, videos, audio tapes and/or CD-ROMs on space, space craft and astronauts.

Books About Space

The Hubble Space Telescope. Diane Sipiera, 1997.

Searching for Alien Life. Is Anyone Out There? Dennis Fradin, 1997.

Space Stations. Diane M. Sipiera and Paul P. Sipiera.

Blast-Off! A Space Counting Book. Norma Cole, 1994.

Stars and Planets. Davis Lambert, 1994.

Where Are the Stars During the Day? Melvin Berger, 1993.

Our Solar System. Seymour Simon, 1992.

The Dream Is Alive. Barbara Emburg, 1990.

Fat Men from Space. Daniel Pinkwater, 1977.

Mars, the Red Planet. Issac Assimov, 1977.

Peterson's First Guide to the Solar System. Jay Pachoff, 1990.

Our Sun and the Inner Planets. Levasseur-Rogourd, 1989.

Miss Pickerell Goes to Mars. Ellen MacGregor, 1951.

Kids Can Make It!

Photocopy rocket on p. 87 onto white construction paper. Have children make rockets according to the directions on p. 84. Attach a string to each rocket and hang from ceiling or staple onto bulletin board.

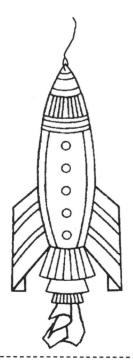

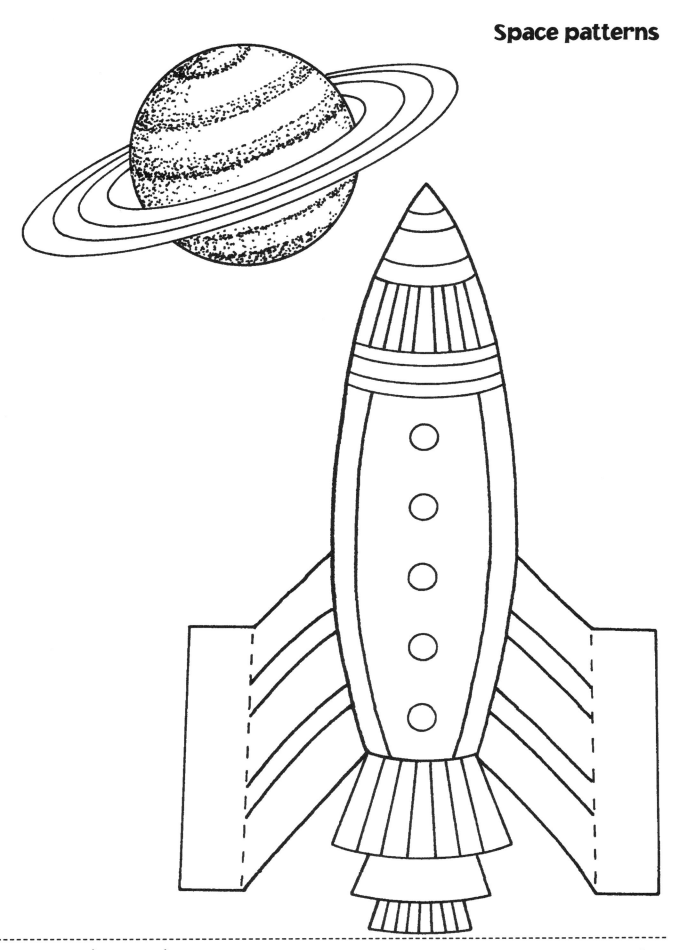